TEMPLE MANAGEMENT

TEMPLE MANAGEMENT

As inspired by Shirdi ke Sai Baba

Dr. Suresh Haware

PRABHAT PRAKASHAN

Published by
PRABHAT PRAKASHAN PVT. LTD.
4/19 Asaf Ali Road,
New Delhi-110 002 (INDIA)
e-mail: prabhatbooks@gmail.com

ISBN 978-93-90923-48-9
TEMPLE MANAGEMENT
by Dr. Suresh Haware

Edition
2025

Price
₹ 500.00 (Rupees Five Hundred only)

Printed at
R-Tech Offset Printers, Delhi

I dedicate this book
with love, affection and devotion
to the fond and loving memories
of Sadguru Shri Sai Baba for inspiration;
to those people with whom I interacted
on the subject of temple management;
and to the temples who will adopt
these principles of management.

Prologue

It could be debated whether God is there or not
but it cannot be ignored that it is the need of the people.

I am happy to present a new book on a very novel subject of temple management. I have served as a nuclear scientist for 27 years. I am in business for the last 25 years and I have served the Sai Baba Sansthan at Shirdi for the last five years as its chairman. With my experience at Shirdi and inspiration from Baba, I would like to state that the scientific approach, the service mind and the management skills have the potential to change the scenario of the temples in India.

India has around 30 lakh temples. It has a potential to bring socio-economic transformation in India. Liberty, equality and fraternity, which are the cardinal principles stated in our Constitution, could be brought about in the society through temples. Temples have a huge potential for employment which has not been harnessed yet.

The temple had been the centre of the village activities. It is also the centre of the human mind. If you look at the social fabric of India, most of the minds are religious, knowingly or unknowingly. Fear and favour are considered to be the two basic tenets that govern the human mind when we talk about the religious behaviour of a person. But apart from this, true *bhakti*, that is, devotion with love and spirituality also impacts the human actions and his behaviour. There are a number of disciples who devote their life in search of God or the truth. Birth, death and marriage are the three important happenings in the life of a man. If these events are connected with the temple, naturally, the citizens get connected and also register with the temples.

You may like to debate whether God is there or not. But when it comes to society and its behaviour, you will realise that it is the need of the people to have a God. Therefore, having a temple(s) in every village is natural. Hence I have proposed an innovative idea of temple management to be adopted by all the temples in India in order to bring about socio-economic transformation in India.

This sounds both logical and practical. The basic facets of management and also called as five M's of management are man, machine, material, market and money. If we were to look at the temple management, all these five principles of management are applicable. Therefore, the aspect of temple management will definitely take shape in the near future. Temples, society, government, institutions: both educational and religious, academicians and citizens will be benefited. It will give a professional touch to the temple.

My emphasis is that the face of the temples should be social. The society and devotee should be the central focus of all temples. It should not give a commercial look which unfortunately is seen in some parts of the country. When we go to a temple, ten fellows will chase us, for this and that and their objective is only to usurp money from us. The very scene will disturb our mind and will generate negative thoughts. We will forget the temple and the deity for a moment–so powerful will be the chase of the people that we may think of giving it up. Anybody will think that this should improve. This underlines the importance and urgency of the concept of temple management.

I was fortunate to get an opportunity to be in close proximity of Baba. With a call from my inner voice and inspiration of Baba, I thought of penning down this book for the benefit of all the temples and citizens of India. I hope that all concerned and mainly the temples and the society will benefit from this book.

Om Sai Ram!!!

Foreword

India has a rich and diverse culture, with its different rituals, practices and customs. The temples all across the country are testimony to such diverse rituals. I am glad that documentation to this effect has come in the form of a book on temple management from a person who has experience of managing the largest temples in India, Dr. Suresh Haware. Being a senior nuclear scientist and a successful businessman besides serving as chairman of Sri Sai Baba temple located at Shirdi, Dr. Haware has penned down his experiences and his prospective plans on managing the temples in India.

Temples in India are an institution in itself and hence require a professional detailing on its planning and optimisation of resources. Sri Sai Baba temple is the second largest temple in India in terms of the footfall of devotees and hence one could visualise the optimum utilisation of its resources. Dr. Haware has keenly observed the systems and processes and has undertaken interventions to improve them further. The book makes an honest attempt to take every stakeholder's expectations into consideration, namely, the management of the temple, devotees, local residents, government authorities and society at large. Further, the book speaks of bringing in professionalism in every aspect of the temple functioning and at the same time also suggests interventions that are social, spiritual and philanthropic in its approach. I am sure this book would serve as a valuable resource to all the stakeholders involved in the management of temples in India.

—Prof. (Dr.) Nitin R. Karmalkar
Hon'ble Vice Chancellor
Savitribai Phule Pune University
Pune, Maharashtra-411007 (India)

Preface

A leader is one who knows the way, goes the way, and shows the way.

—John C. Maxwell[1]

India is a country of temples. There is no village in India that does not have a temple; rather it has a number of them.

30 Lakh Temples

There are around 6.5 lakh (0.65 million) villages in India. While the number of schools and colleges in India is around 20 lakhs (2.0 million), the number of temples in the country is around 30 lakhs (3.0 million). These are only the major temples. If we were to include the small and minor temples, the number may be in crores. It is interesting to observe that the number of temples surpasses the number of schools and colleges. It also gives us an idea about the scale of socio-economic influence that temples exert.

Temple Chains

There is a big diversity in temples' size-small, medium to large ones. Also, there are chains of temples, like ISKCONs, Swaminarayan Akshardham, etc. In terms of funds, many of these temples are financially rich, well established and powerful. Though there is no accurate data available on the income and wealth of the temples, however, some data is collected by the charity commissioners. It is roughly estimated that many of these temples own wealth more than any other industry. Therefore, there is a need for management of these temples; which implies setting up systems and processes.

Employment Potential

Temple management will incorporate professional management in temples. It may be noted that temples possess a huge potential for employment generation that has not yet been harnessed. If qualified human resource is available and employed at the temples, they can inculcate discipline and order in the temple systems. Institutions could carve out professional courses in the subject to make suitable manpower available for the temples. After agriculture and real estate business, that are the first and second largest employers, the temples in India could become the third largest employer.

Temple-centric Towns

In the olden days, the temple used to be the centre of the town. The Meenakshi temple at Madurai is a case in point. Spread over 14 acres of land area, it is located at the centre of the town. All the activities of the town would function around the temple. The temple has good reserves of water, which became the main source of water supply for the town. All individual and family ceremonies would be performed in the temple. In a way, the temple would fulfil all the social needs of the individual. All these temples in India, taken together, generate huge wealth.

An observation of various temples reveals two common shortcomings. Naturally, there are exceptions, but these two shortcomings are generally apparent in temples–the first is that these temples are unorganised, and the second is that they are indisciplined. Of course, there are honourable exceptions. *Darshan* system has to be very well organised. Even the commercial activities around the temple need to be disciplined and many of them could be located at the exit. Therefore, I perceive a need for adopting temple management in order to improve upon the existing setup and provide unique spiritual experience to the devotees.

Temple Wealth

Temples in India are rich in resources. Take, for instance, the Balaji temple at Tirupati, which is the largest temple in India, where the annual receipt is more than Rs. 3,000 crores (Rs. 30 billion). The temple has around 9,000 kg of gold, more than Rs. 14,000 crores of fixed deposits, a total asset of around Rs. 90,000 crores (Rs. 900 billion). It has more than 10,000 employees, the infrastructure is huge and the entire Tirumala Hills are owned by the temple. Their *dharmashalas* can accommodate around 40,000 devotees at a time. They require hundreds of barbers for head tonsuring as hair donation is considered a religious offering. When I enquired about what they do with the hair, I discovered astonishing facts. This donated hair is used to produce the vitamin called 'keratin'. It is also used in the film industry for making wigs. The temple authorities auction the hair and earn more than Rs. 200 crores (Rs. 2 billion) every year. This single instance is sufficient to illustrate the sheer scale of management required in temples. It is managed by three senior IAS cadre officers.

Sai Baba Temple, Shirdi

Now let us consider Shri Sai Baba temple at Shirdi, which is the second largest temple in India. Its annual receipt is around Rs. 700 crores (Rs. 7.0 billion). It has around 5,000 direct employees and provides employment to thousands indirectly. It has a mega kitchen that can feed around one lakh persons every day. This temple-town has around 3,000 big and small hotels and hundreds of restaurants. The temple runs two large hospitals with around 575 beds. On similar lines, we can consider the Golden temple at Amritsar, Vaishnodevi temple at Jammu, Shri Padmanabhaswamy temple at Thiruvananthapuram, the chain of Swaminarayan Akshardham temples, the chain of Hare Rama-Hare Krishna temples, the Jagannath temple in Puri, Siddhivinayak temple in Mumbai, Somnath temple in Gujarat, Sabarimala Ayyappa temple in Kerala, Kashi Vishwanath temple in Varanasi and so on. A temple is no less than an industry if we were to look at the operations involved. The amount of finance involved is huge and so is the employment potential. This phenomenon is unique to India. No other country in the world is so rich in the number of temples or religious places. It is our valuable treasure and an important identity.

Scale of Management

I have served as chairman of the Shri Sai Baba temple trust in Shirdi for five years. I realised that what I have been doing at Shirdi is nothing but temple management. This thought has been inspired by Baba and therefore, *when I talk of temple management, I shall often base my ideas on data and initiatives pertaining to Shri Sai Baba temple at Shirdi. This will help the readers and researchers get a better insight into the scale of management. It will also help readers to understand the importance of management as a profession with reference to the functioning of the temples.*

Professional Management

Nowadays, many temples are managed by IAS cadre officers. Balaji temple at Tirupati (Andhra Pradesh), Shri Sai Baba temple at Shirdi (Maharashtra), Kanak Durga temple at Vijayawada (Andhra Pradesh) are some of the examples of temples that are managed through IAS cadre officers. Let me reiterate that the IAS cadre is trained in handling administration. Though they acquire the tenets of management in the course of their duties, professional management still remains a distinct entity. Therefore, I firmly believe that the temples should be managed by a professional manager, who understands the business. He will be able to inculcate professionalism in temple management.

Scientific and professional management of temples has been neglected in India for centuries (with some honourable exceptions), but the subject is of crucial importance in present time. The purpose of this book is to attract the attention of professionals towards this necessity. If this cannot be done in India, then it cannot be done anywhere else in the world.

I am sure that this book will provide a spark to many minds from the business industry and religious institutions so as to attract many souls to the innovative subject of temple management.

Temple management will make a difference.

Acknowledgement

I sincerely acknowledge the encouragement received from a number of trustees of various temples in India and with whom I discussed the subject of temple management. Their support was so enthusiastic that it made me think of the subject for the last five years. They all agreed to adopt temple management in their activities if they were to get some professional guidance for the same from persons involved in the subject. What has been presented in this book is the extract of this churning of five years on the subject. I also acknowledge the help and support received from Shri Prabhatji, publisher, and I thank him for agreeing to publish a book on this subject. This immediately reminded me of my lovely experience of the last five years of being so close to Baba as chairman of Shri Sai Baba Sansthan Trust, Shirdi, and it compelled me to pen down this book. I would say that it is Baba who inspired me to write on this subject. The editorial team has taken a lot of interest and made the book almost perfect.

I take this opportunity to thank Prof. (Dr.) Nitin R. Karmalkar, Hon'ble Vice Chancellor, Savitribai Phule Pune University, Pune, Maharashtra (India) for accepting my request and writing the foreword for this book. I thank my colleagues at Shirdi for providing valuable inputs and also thank Bhagwan Datar, Gayatri Gadgil, Prashant Suryavanshi and Deepak Kate for the editorial help and support extended by them. I thank all my family members, especially my wife Nalini, sons Amit and Amar, daughters-in-law Richa and Ishaanee and grandchildren Aryan, Aaradhya and Ayana.

Contents

Section-1

General Management

1

Appointment of Board of Trustees

Management is nothing more than motivating other people.

—Lee Iacocca[2]

A temple is an institution. It is mandatory in almost all the states in India to register the temple as a trust with the Charity Commissioner. Therefore, the first agenda of the temple management is the appointment of a Board of Trustees as per the bye-laws of the trust or the Trust Act, if that exists. I have narrated here the circumstances of my appointment and described my first day at the temple. It briefs the readers about the management ideas underlying such a huge establishment.

The provision of appointment in the Act (*see* Appendix-1 for details) is as follows:

1. For the purpose of management of the Sansthan Trust, on or after the appointed day, a Committee to be called "the Shree Sai Baba Sansthan Management Committee" shall be constituted by the State Government.
2. The state government shall, by notification in the *Official Gazette,* appoint, a Chairman, Vice-Chairman and not more than fifteen other members to constitute the Committee: Provided that, out of the total number

of members, not less than one member shall be a woman and one member shall be from the socially and economically weaker section. And provided further that, out of the total number of members, not less than eight members including the Vice-Chairman, shall be persons having educational background with professional or specialised knowledge, qualifications and practical experience in one or more of the fields, such as law, business management, public administration, engineering, architecture, public health, medicine or rural development.

3. The President of the Shirdi *Nagar Panchayat* shall be the *ex-officio* member of the Committee.
4. Subject to the other provisions of this Act, the Committee shall be a body corporate by the name aforesaid, having perpetual succession and a common seal with power to acquire, hold and dispose of property, both movable and immovable, and to contract and shall by the said name sue and be sued.

My Appointment

I was appointed as chairman of the Shri Saibaba Sansthan Trust, Shirdi as per the above-mentioned Act by issuing the *Government Gazette* with the approval of Governor of Maharashtra, on 28th July, 2016. The story of my appointment is interesting. I had visited the Sai Baba temple at Shirdi a few years back. I was standing in the normal queue for *darshan*. The queue was progressing slowly, but a ruckus broke out when I reached near Baba's *samadhi* and I was pushed out of the temple without *darshan*. I was very distressed and immediately told my wife that this was my last visit to Shirdi and that I would never visit Shirdi again. I did not visit Shirdi thereafter. One day, the then Chief Minister of Maharashtra, Hon. Shri Devendra Fadnavis called me and said that he was proposing to appoint me as chairman of Shri Sai Baba Sansthan, Shirdi. I recalled my experience and narrated it to him. He laughed for a while and said, "Perhaps Baba is calling you." Taking this as Sai *prasad*, I decided to accept the responsibility and I joined the temple on 29th July, 2016.

Taking Charge

After the guidance of the then Chief Minister, I left for Shirdi to take charge of the temple management. When I reached Ghoti near Nashik, I received a call from a journalist from Shirdi, suggesting that I cancel my visit. All the shops in Shirdi were closed and the residents of Shirdi had called for a *bandh* (close down for protest). I told him, "I do not leave any of my assignments half way. I shall not cancel my visit. Let Baba's wish prevail. If He so desires, then I shall take charge, otherwise I shall return to Mumbai." To my surprise, by the time I reached Shirdi, everything was fine, all shops were opened and I reached the temple safely. I went around Baba's *samadhi* and took charge of the temple management as chairman.

First Interaction with the Press at Shirdi

Media at Shirdi is very influential and has international reach. Almost all news channels and newspapers have a presence in Shirdi. I addressed the Press after taking charge as chairman. I declared, "The functioning of the temple will be transparent and free from corruption. It will be socially-oriented." One journalist asked me, "We know that you are a busy person; how will you be able to devote time to the temple?" In simple terms, I explained that a person who could perform ten jobs, could also perform eleven. "And a person who is free, who does nothing, can do nothing." The first meeting with the Press was a healthy interaction and it remained the same throughout my tenure in Shirdi.

First Meeting with HoDs

Immediately after the Press interaction, I had a short introductory meeting with all the HoDs. There are 40 departments, each with its own head. There are four administrative officers, one deputy CEO and one CEO (nowadays, s/he is from IAS cadre). After a short introduction, I requested all HoDs to send me an e-mail every evening, briefly describing the work done during the day. I was surprised to learn that only four HoDs knew how to send an e-mail. This marked the beginning of the hurdles. I requested the CEO to train them and I started receiving daily e-mails. Over the entire tenure, the number of e-mails increased from four to 36 but it was never 40.

My First Day at Sai Baba Temple

My plan for my first day at the temple was very simple. I wanted to introduce myself and get to know the temple and the people. Shirdi is a small town but it buzzes with activity. The town's population is around 36,000 (as per the 2011 Census) but it attracts around 70,000 visitors daily. Almost every resident of Shirdi is a businessman. He owns a hotel, a restaurant or a shop. The people are simple, religious and hard working. Their lives revolve around the temple. Shirdi has around 3,000 hotels and around 400 banquets and is popular for destination weddings. It is connected by road, rail and now by air also. More than 28 domestic flights operate daily. The airport has the capacity for night landings and it can receive international flights too. Shirdi airport is one of the busiest airports in India. The temple has around 5,000 employees; accommodation for around 20,000 visitors; around 6,000 students study in the temple-managed educational institutions and the mega kitchen can feed around 1,00,000 devotees every day. It is important to understand the sheer scale of the organisation. I moved around the temple, *dharmashalas*, water reservoirs, *prasadalaya*, schools. I performed *kakad aarti* on the second day and left for Mumbai. It was a hectic day and full of tasks.

□

2

Micro Management

The art of leadership is saying no, not saying yes.
It is very easy to say yes.

—Tony Blair[3]

Micro management is nothing but managing the task by dividing it into small and very small pieces. This is my favourite area of management. It is my practice to take up such micro aspects of management and take immediate decisions on them. This is the beauty of micro management. Let us learn how I implemented it at Shirdi.

Once a job is delegated to them, managers should be given free hand to execute their work. Micro management, as construed by the managers, should be understood in the proper sense. It should not be considered as interference by the leaders in the work of managers. My concept of micro management is limited: the leader only makes a first-hand assessment of the situation and takes instant, practical decisions. Its implementation is then left to the management.

After taking charge at Shirdi, I narrated my experiences and observations of the first day to the then Chief Minister of Maharashtra, Shri Devendra Fadnavis and sought his guidance. I would like the readers to note that he gave me a free hand

and his full support. This is the main reason for my being able to perform so effectively at Shirdi.

First Round of the *Darshan* Queue

On my next visit, after taking Baba's *darshan*, I joined the common *darshan* queue as a devotee and took decisions on two micro items. Each of my visits to Shirdi would begin with Baba's *darshan* and blessings. This was my first round of the *darshan* queue. The authorities were perplexed when I joined the general queue because it had never happened in the past. No chairman had joined the common *darshan* queue like an ordinary devotee. This was happening for the first time. I told them, "There are many things that happen in life for the first time. So, wait and watch."

Direct *Darshan* for Mothers of Infants

One scene in particular affected me deeply. In the midst of the queue, a lady was perched on a bench, hiding her face while she breastfed her infant. She was embarrassed by the crowd of men around her. She could not let her infant go hungry, nor could she give up her place in the queue for *darshan*. The anguish of this mother disquieted me and I resolved that things should be changed urgently. I decided instantly then and there that all such mothers, who carried a child less than two years old need not stand in the queue. Instead, they should be sent for direct *darshan* of Baba. I asked the authorities to implement all my decisions with immediate effect. This was my first decision at Shirdi and I feel proud that Baba inspired me to do that.

Baby-feeding Room

There was an urgent need for creating a baby-feeding room. The authorities immediately identified the space and within one day, a baby-feeding room was set up inside the temple premises.

Senior Citizens

I also observed that there were a number of senior citizens

who were facing discomfort due to waiting and the long walk during the *darshan* queue. They needed to take rest from time to time, but did not do so for fear of losing their place in the queue. So, the next decision I took was to grant direct *darshan* facility for all the senior citizens above the age of 60 years.

Differently-abled (*Divyang*)

As I proceeded in the queue, I observed that there were a number of differently-abled persons in the queue who were feeling discomfort due to the long wait. I ordered to facilitate direct *darshan* for all such devotees. They need not be kept waiting in the queue.

Patients

Similarly, I arranged direct *darshan* for all the patients standing in the queue. The authorities wanted to know how to identify a genuine patient who was eligible for direct *darshan*. It was an important question. I left it to the judgement of the concerned officer in-charge.

Free RO-purified Drinking Water

While in the queue, I noticed that the bottled drinking water was being sold for 15 rupees per bottle; the same bottle that is sold outside for 10 rupees. The temple had given a contract to an agency for this. Why were they charging 15 rupees? Because it is sold in a queue where the devotee cannot leave his/her place. The agents were thus taking undue advantage of the devotees. I decided to do away with this system and arranged for installation of an R.O. (Reverse Osmosis) water plant. We started providing free of cost R.O.-purified drinking water to all the devotees.

Free of Cost Tea and Coffee

Tea and coffee were being sold to devotees waiting in the queue for 2 rupees and 3 rupees respectively. I believed that it was the devotee's right to get tea or coffee while waiting for long in the queue. Therefore, immediately I instructed the authorities to serve it free of cost to all the devotees. I also instructed them to serve milk and biscuits to small children, free of cost. The rate boards displaying the prices were immediately replaced with free of cost signs.

Renovation of Toilets

I also observed that the existing toilet facilities were in very bad shape. I immediately ordered for their renovation to be completed in a few days' time.

Replacement of Flooring

The entire temple premises were floored in Kota stone that had been installed 15 years ago. With heavy wear and tear, it had become uneven and damaged at a number of places. I got the entire flooring replaced with the heavy 35 mm granite stone, that would last for around 50 years.

Light and Ventilation Enhanced

Ventilation in the *darshan* queue was very bad, so was the condition of light. I instructed that the windows be changed and that the number of ceiling fans be doubled. This improved the situation somewhat, but I was far from satisfied.

Air Conditioning for the *Darshan* Queue

I had visualised a ductable air-conditioning system for the queue area. A devotee immediately volunteered to bear the expenses and donated the air-conditioning system to the temple. It was soon installed in the temple at proper locations.

CCTVs

The devotees had nothing to engage themselves with while waiting in the queue for *darshan*. There were a few small size CCTV sets showing live *darshan* of Baba, but their visibility was very poor. They had been installed 15 years ago. I immediately ordered bigger LED TV sets and increased their number to 300, so that the devotee could get Baba's *darshan* from any corner of the queue. This provided good engagement to the devotees.

Surveillance

There are around 310 CCTV cameras installed in various premises of the Sansthan. There is a control room with monitors and round-the-clock surveillance manpower to keep an eye on the happenings to maintain security and discipline.

Udi

Udi prasad is very popular in Shirdi. Devotees do not leave the temple premises without taking this *udi*. *Udi* is the sacred ash produced in the *dhuni* (sacred fire burning since Baba's time) which is continuously burning in *Dwarkamai*. Since the quantity of *udi* produced was less, it was being distributed in a separate queue. I visited the small plant where the *udi* is sieved and packed in a small sachet. They were putting 1.5 g of *udi* in each sachet and thus were able to prepare 50,000 sachets in a day. Since the number of devotees was more than that, there was always a shortage of *udi*. I asked them to fill only 1 g of *udi* in each sachet. Immediately the production went up to 75,000 sachets a day and was more than sufficient for the devotees. Thereafter, *udi* was made available to all the devotees in the same queue after *darshan* and the separate queue was done away with.

Bundi Prasad after *Darshan*

This was an intriguing practice in vogue at the temple– the *bundi prasad* was distributed to the devotees before taking *darshan* of Baba's *samadhi*. The reason behind this was not known. Some devotees would open up the *bundi* packet, start eating it and spill a little bit on the floor. This practice was immediately stopped. Instead, every devotee was given *bundi prasad* after taking *darshan*. The annual cost of this *bundi prasad* was found to be around Rs. 25 crores. On enquiry, I found that every packet of *prasad* contained 100 g of *bundi*. Since it is *prasad* and is therefore symbolic, I directed that the quantity of *bundi* be reduced to 50 g per devotee and the result was a saving of Rs. 12.5 crores annually.

Tilak on Forehead

I noticed that there was a *gandha tilak* on the forehead of a very few persons. I was told that they were VIPs. A *gandha tilak* is such a common thing. If it could make somebody a VIP, then why not make everybody a VIP, I thought. And immediately I decided to place a few persons in the queue to apply *gandha tilak* on everybody's forehead. It made all the devotees proud to be treated like VIPs.

Recycling Flowers to make *Agarbatti*

I observed that around 3 to 3.5 tonnes of flowers were offered on the *samadhi* of Baba every day. I asked the authorities as to what they did with the flowers. The answer disturbed me. The flowers were being thrown into garbage. I thought that this was dishonouring the devotees' feelings and emotions attached to these flowers. My mind remained disturbed for days together until we arrived at the idea of recycling these flowers into *agarbatti* (incense sticks). This item is covered in detail in a separate chapter towards the end of the book. It is interesting to note that this became a startup venture with an annual turnover of Rs. 5 crores. A very illuminating case study!

VIP *Darshan* Pass without Recommendation

After coming out of the *Samadhi Mandir*, I visited the PRO office, which was always crowded. They were busy issuing the VIP *darshan* passes. These special passes were being issued only to those who had a letter of recommendation from MLAs, MPs or ministers. Though the passes cost only Rs. 200/- each, they were being sold in the market for Rs. 1,000/. I immediately decided to do away with the system of recommendation. The results were a pleasant shock to everyone. This has been described in detail in this book in a chapter on *Darshan* Management.

Sai *Paduka* Engraved on a Silver Coin

Next, I looked for the donation counters. They were

located in a corner with no ventilation and poor lighting. Donors were made to stand in a long queue to make donations. The employees at the donation counters were too busy to even look up and see the faces of the devotees. They were just not bothered. I asked the authorities what was the take away for the devotees after giving donation? How did they honour the donors? The authorities were awestruck as they had been asked this for the first time. I asked them to shift the donation counters near to the *samadhi* temple. The new, airy and well-lit counters would resemble a corporate office, because this was the place where the income for the temple was being generated. I also instructed that some employees should welcome and honour the donors with flowers. I decided that any donor donating more than Rs. 25000/-, would be offered a return gift–a pair of Sai Baba's *paduka* in the form of a silver coin. It took some time to make these coins available, but receiving Baba's *paduka* as a gift from the temple made the donors emotional. They felt as though they were taking home Baba with them.

Ladoo Prasad

Ladoo prasad being distributed was limited and there was a long queue for getting the *bundi ladoo prasad*. Each devotee was given only one packet. So if a devotee wanted three packets of *prasad*, s/he needed to stand in the queue three times. Each packet contained three *ladoos* made of *bundi* and cost Rs. 25/-. The annual *ladoo* production was 2.5 lakh *ladoos*. I decided that the production of *bundi ladoo prasad* should be doubled. We subsidised its cost by 20 per cent and allowed the devotees to take as many packets of *prasad* as they wanted. This eased out the queue and enhanced the happiness of the devotees.

Waiting Facility for *Darshan*

When I came out of the temple complex, I found that there were many devotees waiting for their turn to join the queue. I visualised that there should be a proper waiting complex for the devotees so that they would not be made to wait in the sun and rain. So, we designed the ultra-modern *darshan* queue complex. This is described in detail in a separate chapter in this book. Again a very interesting chapter!

Biometric Computerised Time Slots for *Darshan*

I was astonished to find that each devotee took an average of six to seven hours to get *darshan*. I decided to work on this and employ technology to reduce their waiting time. With the implementation of biometric computerised time-slot *darshan* facility, the *darshan* time was reduced to just half an hour per devotee. Yes, half an hour! This is described in detail in a separate chapter in this book; a successful exercise on time management and hence a must- read item!

Thus, my joining the *darshan* queue provided succor and immense satisfaction to thousands of devotees. When I ask myself, as the chairman of the temple; 'what is my main job?' The immediate answer that comes to my mind is 'to provide quick, pleasant and satisfactory *darshan* experience to the devotees'. This is my primary duty and all other jobs are secondary. I find that I have largely, though not fully, succeeded in this.

□

3

Macro Management

Those who plan do better than those who do not plan even though they rarely stick to their plan.

—Winston Churchill[4]

Macro management is not just looking at things superficially; it is about making decisions regarding the major projects. Large temples will face the need of macro management. The services of the temple depend on the number of devotees visiting the temple on a daily basis. Power, water, food, prasad, lodging, transportation, communication, website, digital platforms, even online arrangements for *darshan*, donation, *pooja* schedule, literature and so on–each of these services at a temple like Shirdi are obviously on a large scale, like an industry.

PM at Shirdi

For example, during the visit of the Hon'ble Prime Minister Narendra Modi to Shirdi, the projects worth 575 crores were initiated and *bhumi pujan* of these projects was performed. These included the construction of a modern educational complex spanning over 7.0 lakh sq.ft. worth Rs. 218 crores, the 10 MWe solar power plant worth Rs. 40 crores, the *Darshan*

Queue Complex worth Rs. 120 crores and the Sai Knowledge Park worth Rs. 197 crores.

Healthcare Improvement

There are two hospitals at Shirdi owned by Saibaba Sansthan, viz Sainath Hospital and Saibaba Hospital. Sainath is a general hospital with 325 beds and Saibaba is a super speciality hospital with 250 beds. The machinery and equipment at these hospitals were purchased 15 years ago. The service contracts for the machinery were costing more than their depreciation value. Therefore, it was the right time to decide to scrap them and buy new ones. Technology changes every five years. The purchase of new and state-of-the-art machinery is required to keep the facilities up-to-date and provide the best service to the beneficiaries. Therefore, it was decided to scrap around 128 such machines and buy new ones, including CT Scan, MRI and Cath lab. All these were purchased and the hospitals were upgraded. More details of this are given in a separate chapter on hospitals.

Water Scarcity

Though very close to Godavari river in Kopargaon, Shirdi has to face water scarcity for almost the entire year. Unlike other parts of Maharashtra, Shirdi gets an average annual rainfall of only around 200 mm. The Konkan region gets around 3,000 mm. The Vidarbha region gets around 1,200 mm of rainfall. Mumbai gets around 2,500 mm of rainfall. At times, Mumbai sees more than 200 mm of rainfall in a day which is similar to the annual rainfall of 200 mm in Shirdi. In the months of April and May, Shirdi has to depend on water supply from tankers. With proper planning it is now made tanker-free. Therefore, water management became an essential activity in Shirdi, which is again discussed in a separate chapter in this book.

Lodging Facilities

Saibaba Sansthan has lodging facilities to accommodate around 20,000 devotees. All these facilities need to be kept updated. They had not been renovated for a long time. The regular upkeep of the buildings enhances the life of the buildings and provides better service to the devotees. I decided to renovate all these buildings, one by one. The plumbing had become so old that it was eroded at places and leakages/ seepages had started. The electrical network and even the wiring had given up. The 60 wattage incandescent bulbs were replaced with 10-watt LED bulbs, which helped reduce the power consumption to just one-sixth. It became part of my job to visit these facilities on a regular interval.

Mega Kitchen

The solar-operated mega kitchen of the Sansthan also required a number of changes. The kitchen at Tirupati cooks only rice for the devotees; at Shirdi, however, it is necessary to serve *chapatis*, considering the food preferences of the devotees. Making *chapati* is an art, common in Indian households. There are no coaching classes that teach *chapati* making. It is mostly learned at home, from the parents. Nearly 70 thousand to one lakh devotees eat at Shirdi every day and the requirement of *chapatis* for them is proportionately huge. They have to be made on a large scale. So, we had to get a *chapati*-making machine specially designed to meet this requirement. This was possible only in Punjab. So, we got two such machines which can make 25,000 *chapatis* in an hour. These are perfectly round in shape, roasted on both the sides and applied with *ghee*. The machines are worth visiting, when you go to Shirdi next time.

Education

Saibaba Sansthan manages five educational institutions which include Girls School, English-medium School from KG to 10th, Junior College, Senior College and ITI. More than 6,000 students are studying in these institutions. This will give an idea of the scale of their operation. I wanted to interact with the students of 10th and 12th class. They were around 1,000 in number. The authorities did not know where to assemble all these students because all the schools were running in the *dharmashalas*. It was a makeshift arrangement and had continued for years together. Finally, the meeting was arranged in the corridor of the school premises, without proper seating arrangements. All students were sitting on the floor, that too at two different levels. There were a number of pillars obstructing the view. Only 200 of the 1,000 students could be accommodated. I had a very enjoyable interaction with the students. Later, some parents conveyed their appreciation to me regarding the interaction–it was the first such interaction in the history of Shirdi. What struck me was that the students were not getting the experience of an educational institution. I envisioned and commissioned the design for a modern educational complex, spanning over 7.0 lakh square feet of area and equipped with all the modern facilities for sports, library, laboratory, assembly, indoor and outdoor sports, swimming pool and an auditorium with a capacity of 1,200, for academic and cultural programmes. Shirdi attracts a number of visitors from the industry, films, literary circles, IAS, politicians, judges and other dignitaries. Many of them could be requested to interact with the students. Very soon, this could become possible in our modern educational complex which is nearing completion (read more about this complex in a separate chapter on education).

Waste Management

Waste management was a subject of utmost importance at Shirdi and was also very close to my heart. I thought of making Shirdi clean and green. On 2nd October, 2016, I wanted to arrange a cleaning drive with the help of students, employees, citizens and devotees. I organised a meeting to discuss this issue. Everyone was enthused about participating in the programme. The senior citizens of Shirdi raised a very vital issue. They said, "It is good to clean Shirdi, we like it, but the question is where to dump the garbage?" The information they revealed was shocking. The solid waste was being dumped near borders of Shirdi so far, but with the expansion of the town, that area too had been occupied. Then they found the six wells which were dried up and had started dumping waste in these wells, one by one. Over a period of time, all the wells were filled up with garbage. Now they had no place to dump the garbage. On this count, the cleaning drive of 2nd October had to be given up. But the thought of where to dump the garbage persisted in my mind. I started looking at scientific literature and technological solutions. Ultimately, I narrowed down to anaerobic bio-digestion of the garbage in a digester, producing methane gas and then electricity. I studied the subject in depth and was convinced that the waste was not really a waste; it could be converted into wealth. Waste management is a commercially viable proposition. I wanted to install a model in Shirdi to prove my conviction. This project was designed, the site was finalised, tenders were invited and my tenure at Shirdi came to an end. I understand that it is being pursued by the Sansthan. (This project is covered in detail in a separate chapter in this book).

New Projects

New projects, new schemes, new initiatives have to be envisioned. Policy decisions have to be taken. A large number of devotees pour into Shirdi every day. They donate with love and affection. Resources are generated automatically. The Sansthan's procedure for spending has been made very clumsy and time-consuming. The Sansthan also lacks the expertise to get things planned, designed and then execute them. The donations made to the temple cannot be spent in a right manner. The Sansthan is run in surpluses, and possessed around Rs. 2,500 crores as fixed deposits. As per the law, the Sansthan had to spend 85 per cent of the income in the same year, failing which, it was to be taxed. This did not actually happen. There is a provision made by the income-tax authorities that even if such money remains unspent, it will be carried forward for the next five years; it will not be taxed.

It will, however, be taxed in the sixth year. Unutilised money was getting accumulated at the Sansthan. I tried to utilise maximum funds for planned projects, but I faced the hurdles of the complicated procedures, inertia of the government machinery, lack of expertise in the Sansthan and over-activism by RTI and PIL activists. Finally, my assessment was that the Sansthan would end up in paying taxes on unutilised funds every year to the government.

Such is the importance of macro management. We have seen how both micro and macro management are beneficial. Let us move to a new section on administrative management. □

Section-2

Administrative Management

4

Human Resource Management

Get the right people. Then no matter what all
else you might do wrong after that,
the people will save you.
That's what management is all about.

—Tom DeMarco[5]

What is a Human Resource[6]?

It may feel a bit weird to refer to people as 'human resources'. Human resources are all the people who in one capacity or another, work for or contribute to an organisation. These people make up a company's workforce. They can be regular employees, for example, but also contractors. Especially with the rise of the gig economy, more and more people are starting to work for an organisation on a contractual basis without having a traditional labour contract. These people include independent contractors, workers provided by contract firms, on-call workers, and temporary help agency workers.

What is Human Resource Management?

Let's start with a brief definition. Human Resource Management, or HRM, is the practice of managing people to achieve better performance. For example, if we were to hire people in a business, we would look for people who can fit the company culture as they would be happier, stay longer and be more productive than people who do not fit into the company culture. Another example is engagement. Engaged employees are more productive, deliver higher-quality work and make customers happier. This means that if we can find ways to make employees more engaged, we can help the company. This is what Human Resource Management boils down to: optimising company performance through better management of human resources. The next question is, who are these Human Resources? An independent contractor can be under contract for years in the same organisation, while an agency worker can work for 20 different companies throughout the year. Because these people are all involved in the company to a different extent, the way they are managed and involved in the organisation should also be different. In addition, there are increasingly non-humans at work in the company. In this case, we're talking about the increase in robotisation. Robots are increasingly involved in day-to-day work and interaction between man and machine is becoming increasingly essential for the success of the organisation. They are used for cleaning and other jobs. Although these machines are not considered 'human resources', there is a case to be made that they should be included in some way as they are part of the workforce.

The Seven HR Basics

When we talk about Human Resource Management, there are a number of elements that are considered cornerstones for effective HRM policies. These cornerstones are:

1. Recruitment and selection
2. Performance management
3. Learning and development
4. Succession planning
5. Compensation and benefits
6. Human Resources Information Systems
7. HR data and analytics

At Shirdi

The temple has around 2,500 permanent employees and around 3,500 employees who are working on contract basis. Though they are on contractual basis, they have been working for the Sansthan for more than 15 years. Every year the contractor changes, but the employees remain the same. In addition to this, there are thousands of employees of various agencies who work for the temple, for example, security or house-keeping, etc. These are the primary employees. There is secondary and tertiary employment by way of shop-keepers, hoteliers, travel agents and so on. On considering the hotels and restaurants in Shirdi which are around 3,000 in number and their employees, we will realise that the town of Shirdi is no less than an industrial township. The temple generates huge employment opportunities and a large amount of economic activity. Just take the example of flowers offered at the *samadhi* of Sai Baba. Around 3 to 3.5 tonnes of flowers are offered daily. These are grown in and around Shirdi in nearly 50 villages. Hundreds of farmers grow flowers and sell them in the wholesale market in Shirdi. There is a flower *mandi* (auction) that is held every morning. The shop-keepers and makers of garlands, bouquets etc. are hundreds in number. Nowadays, the temple, in collaboration with an NGO, has installed an industrial unit for conversion of these flowers into incense sticks (*agarbatti*). This seemingly simple flower offering generates employment for thousands of people.

Employees' Welfare

All the permanent employees are paid a good salary. During my tenure, I decided to improve their salary as per the Seventh Pay Commission recommendations and the same has been implemented. The employees on contract basis were paid a meagre amount of salary, say around Rs. 5,000/- to 6,000/- per month. Many of them had been working on this salary for more than a 15 years. Most of them were married and living with children and parents. It was difficult for them to meet their expenses. I immediately decided to give them an interim relief by way of a 40 per cent increase in their pay. Also, I sanctioned them a paid weekly holiday, reimbursement of tuition fees for their children, included them in the insurance scheme, allowed them and their families to avail free treatment at the hospitals run by the temple and also sanctioned them an advance up to Rs. 1,00,000/- in case they were required to be admitted to some other hospital. Later, I decided to make them permanent employees and also to implement the Seventh Pay Commission scale for these employees who were working on contract basis. These measures generated a wave of happiness among the employees and gave them a very high level of job satisfaction.

Forty Departments

All these employees are divided to work in 40 departments under the HoD or head of the department. They work at hospitals, schools, temples, mega kitchen, water supply, power supply, *dharmashalas*, security, CCTV and surveillance, house-keeping, construction and maintenance, gardens, transport, firefighting, computers and data management, donation counters, *ladoo prasad, udi prasad* and so on. Every year, training courses are arranged to upgrade their skills. Though these employees live in a small town like Shirdi, they impart good services to the devotees pouring in from the entire country and also from various corners of the world.

Four Pillars

The villagers, trustees, devotees and employees are the four pillars of the Sai Baba temple in Shirdi. The village population is around 36,000 (as per the 2011 Census data). Another 20,000 from the adjoining villages throng Shirdi every day along with about 60 to 70 thousand devotees. While employees are in round-the-clock service to the devotees, the Board of Trustees takes decisions on policies and everyday necessities. At times, a conflict of interest does occur; this is when the Board of Trustees plays a pivotal role in mitigating the disputes and differences. For example, the Board of Trustees decided to take Sai Baba's original *paduka* around the country for *darshan* by the devotees spread across the nation. A section of the villagers were opposed to taking out the original *paduka*, instead they wanted the replica in silver to be taken around. Their main contention was that if *paduka* were taken to different places, the devotees would get *darshan* in their hometown and the number of devotees visiting Shirdi would be reduced. This would affect the businesses at Shirdi. The differences were amicably resolved by holding a number of deliberations with the Trustees and the original *paduka* were taken out in a specially-designed chariot (*rath*) to various parts of the country. The effect was contrary to what the villagers had feared. In Baba's Samadhi Centenary Year, the number of devotees visiting Shirdi increased to 3.5 crore in a year as compared to the usual 2.5 crores per year. I would like to add here that my tenure at Shirdi was full of activities and a number of disputes and differences occurred among the four pillars. These differences were amicably resolved, a good deal of cohesiveness was achieved and all the programmes were celebrated together with enthusiasm.

Living Element

Out of all the five aspects of management, people are the main aspect and they are the only living element. All others are non-living and can be taken care of. Therefore, HR management plays a very important role in management and also in temple management. Productivity can be increased or decreased, depending upon the support of the employees. To be more productive and more profitable, we need to approach this aspect of management in a more humane way.

□

5

Local Management

Management is doing things right;
leadership is doing the right things.

—Peter Drucker[7]

Shirdi Nagar Panchayat

Nagar Panchayat is the local civic management body of the government of Maharashtra. The managing committee of the Nagar Panchayat is a publicly-elected body of representatives. Their chief is called the chairman of the Nagar Panchayat. As per the constitution of Shri Sai Baba Sansthan Trust, Shirdi, the chairman of the Nagar Panchayat is the sitting member of the Board of Trustees of the Sansthan. He attends all the Board meetings as a representative of the Shirdi town and helps in coordination between the Sansthan and the Panchayat. Both these organisations work closely together and fulfill the purpose of providing good civic infrastructure facilities to the devotees. Such a big temple is at the core of the economy of this particulár town. Hence the management of the temple and the local authorities should work hand in hand for the projects of common interest.

Shirdi Town

The devotees coming to Shirdi outnumber the population

of Shirdi. Though farming had been the main occupation of the villagers of Shirdi, with the evolution of Shirdi as a commercial centre, the locals of Shirdi have developed the acumen for doing business. There are around 3,000 hotels and restaurants in Shirdi and around 5,000 shops. All of these, except a few, are owned by the locals. Though a majority of them are given to operators to run the business, the owners keep a close supervision on a day-to-day basis. Thus, the town of Shirdi has now become a commercial hub in the Nagar district and the surrounding townships.

Development of Shirdi

Shirdi has been dependent on the temple, rather than the government, for its development. Most of the roads in Shirdi, the sewage treatment plant, the water supply scheme for Shirdi, the cleaning of Shirdi township on daily basis–all of these are activities are carried out with the help and financial support of the temple. The Sansthan has provided the fire tender for the town to the Nagar Panchayat. The Nagar Panchayat does not impose any taxes on the devotees and largely depends on the Sansthan for the funds required for development. They present their requirements before the Board of Trustees of the Sansthan. I recall that, in my tenure, I had accepted all the proposals of the Nagar Panchayat and had sanctioned more than Rs. 329 crores for various development activities.

The Press in Shirdi

Shirdi has a powerful Press, both print and electronic media. Almost all the newspapers and news channels have a presence in Shirdi. The news from Shirdi garners interest in all the corners of the world. Every day, VIPs and celebrities pour into Shirdi for Sai Baba's *darshan* and that makes the news. Also, it is a politically vibrant town. The Press is busy covering news all the time. There is a good spirit of friendship among the reporters and they share the news so that ultimately it spreads all over the world.

Police in Shirdi

Maharashtra Police has a good set-up in Shirdi township to ensure the safety and security of the devotees and citizens. Barring a few incidents, the township of Shirdi is peaceful. The locals are law-abiding. However, there are complaints about pickpockets. A surprising fact came to my notice that there are a number of inter-state teams of pickpockets, at least 15 in number, with a presence in Shirdi. Shirdi Police are aware of this and are capable of controlling them, if they wish.

Shirdi Airport

Shirdi International Airport was inaugurated by the President of India Hon'ble Shri Ramnath Kovind on 1st October, 2017–it was also the day of the inauguration of Sai Baba's Samadhi Centenary celebrations. The airport, which started with daily two flights from Hyderabad, now has 28 flights daily from 10 destinations, like Delhi, Jaipur, Hyderabad, Chennai, Bangalore, Mumbai, Bhopal, etc. It is the third busiest airport in Maharashtra, after those of Mumbai and Pune. The airport is located in Kakadi village, 14 kms from Shirdi and it was built with partial financial support from the Sai Baba Sansthan. The runway was 2,500 m to begin with and has been extended to 3200 m, so that international flights can be operated. Recently, night-landing facilities have been provided so that the airport can operate 24x7.

Shirdi Railway

Sainagar railway station, located 4 kms from the temple, is the official railway station of Shirdi. Around 58 trains per week operate to and from Shirdi. The pilgrim centres, like Tirupati, Jagannath Puri, Pandharpur, Shegaon are connected with Shirdi by railways. Recently, a superfast train between Mumbai and Shirdi was introduced. When Hon'ble Railway Minister Mr. Piyush Goyal visited Shirdi, we proposed to integrate Sai *darshan* with the railway booking facility through IRCTC. He accepted the proposal and in a short time the facility was launched. Now, if you book a railway ticket from anywhere to Shirdi, a window will pop up, asking if you want to book Sai *darshan*. With the payment of Rs. 200/- per ticket one can instantly book VIP *darshan* along with the railway ticket.

Shirdi by Road

Shirdi is connected to all the parts of the country by road via Nashik, Pune and Mumbai. Majority of the pilgrims visit Shirdi by road. State Transport buses as well as private passenger vehicles operate from various destinations. Many devotees drive their own vehicles to visit Shirdi. Devotees can plan their tour at any time as per their convenience. Devotees have the strong belief that they do not go to Shirdi, but are called by Sai Baba to visit Shirdi. Therefore, we find that the majority of the visits are unplanned. Devotees simply get up and head to Shirdi.

Destination Weddings

Recently, Shirdi has become a wedding destination of choice for many couples. Shirdi has around 400 banquet halls of different sizes with suitable infrastructure. This destination wedding becomes a memorable event for the hosts as well as the guests. The corporate world also has started hosting conferences and workshops at Shirdi. This is a growing business and has good potential.

Shirdi and Around

Shani Shingnapur, the famous Shani Mandir is the nearest to Shirdi. Newase, where Saint Dnyaneshwar wrote *Dnyaneshwari,* his famous commentary on *Srimad Bhagavad Gita,* is also nearby. Nashik and Trimbakeshwar, famous for its Shiva temple which is one of the 12 holy *jyotirlingas*, are also nearby. There are a number of tourist attractions and infotainment centres in Shirdi which could keep one engaged for days together.

Pilgrimage Centre

Shirdi is considered as an important pilgrimage centre

in India, where the devotees pour in from all over the world. Many celebrities from the film industry, business, politics, judiciary, sports, etc. visit Shirdi on a regular basis.

Management of all these local institutions is an important aspect of temple management. All of them have their own defined management but there needs to be good coordination among them. Ultimately, everything revolves around the temple and almost all these agencies are helping the Sansthan to perform better.

□

6
Management of Board Meetings

Arise! Awake! And stop not until the goal is reached.

—Swami Vivekanand[8]

Board of Trustees/Directors is the supreme authority in any organisation. There is a predefined methodology for the working of the Board. It is a normal practice to offer meeting allowance and transport allowance to the Trustees/Directors. This is normally resolved in the first meeting or prior to that. When the subject was raised at our first Board meeting, instead of putting the same for discussion, I wrote in the register that I will not take either a meeting allowance or any transport allowance and signed the register. When the same register was circulated, every member of the Board followed suit and unanimously decided not to take the allowances. An apparently small and simple act, but it would go a long way and would have a positive impact, for this was the first act that showed the selfless working of the Trustees. Such things are very important when one considers the working of a temple in the larger context of public life.

Notice

Notice of the meeting with the agenda is sent to all the members either seven or 15 days in advance as per the

Act/ Board guidelines. Advance notice of seven clear days is required to be given to the Trustees as per Shri Saibaba Sansthan Trust Act, along with the agenda items and detailed notes. It is the mandate that the interval between the two consecutive meetings of the Board should not be of more than 30 days. Every organisation has a normal practice of meeting at least once every month. There are items of policy decisions and of administrative nature, all of which need the approval of the Board. However, items worth some prefixed amount may have to be sent to the higher body, Scrutiny Committee and/or the government for approval, as provided in the Act/ Guidelines. Also, in some organisations, the CEO is authorised to spend some fixed amount (less than Rs.3.0 lakhs in Sai Sansthan) for emergency purposes, but it requires post-facto sanction from the Board.

Detailed Notes

The agenda item should be accompanied with detailed notes on the subject matter. It should narrate in brief the background of the subject, the need for the subject, the finances involved, estimates and the budget provisions, the impact of the subject, the opinion of the administration on the subject matter, government approvals if in place and so on. If the Sai Baba Sansthan wishes to procure anything costing above Rs. 3.0 lakhs, it is mandatory to follow the e-tendering process that is designed and instituted by the government of Maharashtra. I am of the opinion that it is a transparent system and should be adopted by all the temples to avoid manipulations. In case of some small temples, the limit could be brought down to Rs. 1.0 lakh.

Rules and Regulations

Every institution has its own rules and regulations to be followed by all. Officers of the Sansthan would attend the Board meeting and assist the Board with the updated rules and regulations. Any query by the members of the Board would be instantly resolved by the administrative officers, so that it helps in making a thoughtful decision.

Conducting Meetings

The chairman of the Board presides over the Board meetings and in his absence, the vice-chairman presides. The designated officer would read the titles of the subjects, one by one and with the permission of the Chair, members would express their opinion. Usually, each meeting would begin with the confirmation of the minutes of the previous meeting and it would be followed by the agenda of the day's meeting. Sometimes, urgent matters crop up after sending the agenda to the members. These urgent items can be taken up for discussion by the Board with the permission of the Chair. In Sai Baba Sansthan, every meeting, mandatorily begins with Baba's *aarti*.

Members are supposed to address the chairman and any cross-discussion amongst the members should be avoided. Members can raise queries for further information about the subject, if required. The concerned officers are also invited to attend the Board meeting for the part of their subject only. They have to provide the information sought by the Board and can participate in the meeting. However, they have to leave the meeting once their agenda item is over. The chairman is supposed to conduct the meeting in an impartial and peaceful manner. Everyone present contributes to the subject and when the matter is decided, it is considered as a mature, learned and cautious decision, since many heads are involved in the process.

For some agenda items, it is necessary to call outside agencies, consultants and sometimes even presentations related to the subject matter are made by them. It is not necessary to decide on each matter on the spot. Ideally each matter should be decided immediately, but sometimes, it needs to be deferred for want of more information.

Convening and conducting a Board meeting is a

specialised job and should be done by experienced persons. I believe that the minutes of the meetings should be written in an impersonal manner without naming who said what. This is very important as it is the Board that is responsible for the decision and not the individual member. If the minutes are written in the manner of who said what and if a controversy arises, then a particular person could be targeted by the public.

Decision-Making[9]

Decision-making is the thought process of choosing from a set of alternatives. Every decision-making process produces an outcome that might be an action, a recommendation, or an opinion. Since doing nothing or remaining neutral is among the set of options one chooses from, selecting that course is also equivalent to making a decision. I would recall here Hon'ble Mr. Narsimha Rao who was the Prime Minister of India. He was famous for not taking any decisions and he once commented that no decision is also a decision.

Difference between Problem Analysis and Decision-Making

While they are related, problem analysis and decision-making are distinct activities. Decisions are commonly focused on a problem or a challenge. Decision-makers must gather and consider data before making a choice. Problem analysis involves framing the issue by defining its boundaries, establishing criteria with which to select from alternatives, and developing conclusions based on available information. Analysing a problem may not result in a decision, although the results of the analysis are an important ingredient in all decision-making.

Steps in Decision-Making

Decision-making comprises a series of sequential activities that together structure the process and facilitate its conclusion. These steps are:

- Establishing objectives

- Classifying and prioritising objectives
- Developing selection criteria
- Identifying alternatives
- Evaluating alternatives against the selection criteria
- Choosing the alternative that best satisfies the selection criteria
- Implementing the decision

Analysis of Alternatives

Too many choices increase the difficulty of making a decision. A major part of decision-making is the analysis of a defined set of alternatives against selection criteria. These criteria usually include costs and benefits, advantages and disadvantages and alignment with preferences. For example, when choosing a place to establish a new business, the criteria might include rental costs, availability of skilled labour, access to transportation and means of distribution, and proximity to customers. Based on the relative importance of these factors, a business owner makes a decision that best meets the criteria.

The decision-maker may face a problem when trying to evaluate alternatives in terms of their strengths and weaknesses. This can be especially challenging when there are many factors to consider. Time limits and personal emotions also play a role in the process of choosing between alternatives. Greater deliberation and information-gathering often takes additional time, and decision-makers often must choose before they feel fully prepared. In addition, the more that is at stake, the more emotions are likely to come into play, and this can distort one's judgement.

Minutes of the Meeting

It is said in a lighter vein that a meeting is where hours are wasted and minutes are kept. (It is also said that decisions are taken in the corridors and only endorsed in a Board meeting). Apart from the joke, it is true that the outcome of every meeting would be the minutes. It is a practice to send the minutes of the earlier meeting to all the members along with the agenda for the next meeting. They are taken up for discussion and confirmation. In effect, the members are given one more opportunity to add something, to check the correctness of the writing or to suggest some corrections. Confirmation of the minutes of the earlier meeting is normally the first item of the agenda at the Board meeting. The person taking down the minutes should be skilled enough in shorthand.

Confirmation of Minutes

Unless the minutes of the earlier meeting are confirmed, with some exceptions, they are not to be sent for execution of decisions.

Uploading Decisions on Website

Decisions of the meeting after confirmation are to be uploaded on the Sansthan website so that they are in the public domain, i.e. the devotees and the public can access them. This helps in maintaining transparency. The day of the Board meeting would be very eventful. Interested parties would throng around to know the decisions. They would download the relevant decisions from the website of the Sansthan.

Execution of Decisions

Following the practice of uploading all such decisions on the official website of the Sansthan, the Board decisions are then given to the particular departments for execution. However, the Board, through officers, keeps an eye on the progress of the execution of all the decisions.

Policy Decisions

Some decisions are of the nature of a policy; they have a long lasting and wide impact, for example, implementation of Seventh Pay Commission scales to all the employees. Such decisions of the Board may be required to be sent to the Scrutiny Committee and/or government for approval. Unless such approval is obtained, these decisions cannot be implemented.

Administrative Decisions

Some decisions are of a routine administrative nature. They can be decided then and there and can be instantly put for action. These would form more than 50 per cent of all the decisions taken in the Sai Baba Sansthan.

□

7

Execution of Decisions

Average people have great ideas;
legends have great execution.

—Unknown[10]

The execution of decisions is the most crucial activity in any organisation for fulfilling the intent of the decision. Unless the decision is executed, it has no meaning.

Strategy Execution[11]

Although strategy is important, it is pretty much worthless without execution. So let us learn what strategy execution is?

Strategy execution is a process. The most notable book to date on strategy execution is *Execution: The Discipline of Getting Things Done,* by Larry Bossidy and Ram Charan. Bossidy, a retired CEO, and Charan, a renowned management consultant, make the case for execution as a discipline or 'systematic way of exposing reality and acting on it.' They explain that 'the heart of execution lies in three core processes':

1. People
2. Strategy
3. Operations

They explain the processes and descriptions managers use to successfully drive business results.

Strategy Execution as a System

The information presented in the aforementioned book is certainly useful, but the authors do not fully explain how an organisation can implement their three-core processes to achieve strategy success. There have been significant advancements in this area since *Execution...* was published in 2002. In 2008, Harvard Business School's Professor Robert S. Kaplan and his Palladium Group colleague David P. Norton wrote: *The Execution Premium: Linking Strategy to Operations for Competitive Advantage.* In it they presented their management system, which houses six sequential stages intended to help organisations capture what they call an 'execution premium'–a measurable increase in value derived from successful strategy execution. They outline six stages in this system:

1. Develop the strategy
2. Plan the strategy
3. Align the organization
4. Plan operations
5. Monitor and learn
6. Test and adapt

Through detailed sub-activities–26 in total–Kaplan and Norton explain how organisations have successfully executed strategy via application of their management system.

Strategy Execution as a Decision-making Process

Both the models outlined above are important and anyone serious about the practice of strategy execution should be familiar with them. But both do not focus on what I believe to be most important. The one definition that so far resonates most with me is the one by Jeroen de Flander. His explanation of strategy execution starts with a famous quote by Mintzberg:

Strategy is a pattern in a stream of decisions. — Henry Mintzberg

First, there is the overall decision–the big choice–that guides all other decisions. To make a big choice, we need to decide who we want to focus on–our target client segment–and we need to decide how we can offer unique value to the customers in our chosen segment. That is basic business strategy stuff.

By formulating it this way, it helps us to better understand the second part, the day-to-day decisions–the small choices–that get us closer to the finish line. When these small choices are in line with the big choice, we get a Mintzberg Pattern. So if strategy is a decision pattern, strategy execution enables people to create a decision pattern. In other words:

Strategy execution is helping people make small choices in line with a big choice.–Jeroen Flander

This notion requires a big shift in the way we typically think about execution. Looking at strategy execution, we should imagine a decision tree rather than an action plan. Decision patterns, not to-do lists, are at the core of successful strategy journeys.

To improve the strategy implementation quality, we should shift our energy from asking people to make action plans; instead, we can help them make better decisions.

At Shirdi

The decisions taken by the Board, after confirmation of the minutes and upon obtaining approval of the higher body, if required, are sent to various divisions for execution. The process of execution of the decisions is predefined in all the organisations as per their regular practice. SOPs or standard operating procedures are to be followed while executing the decisions. Administrative decisions are quick to be implemented whereas the policy decisions take a little longer. They may require further deliberations at a higher level in the management. Execution of decisions is a continuing process. It may involve raising a tender or inviting quotations, if the task is smaller. Accordingly, the time taken for execution may vary. If it is an e-tender, it is mandatory that it receives three valid quotations and the lowest or L-1 is selected. If it receives less than three quotations, the e-tender has to be raised again. This time, even if it receives two valid quotations, it could be considered. And if it has to be raised for a third time, then even if it receives a single valid quotation, the same can be considered as per the procedure laid down by the government of Maharashtra.

Delegate but do not Forget

I had developed a methodology at Shirdi to assess the implementation of decisions though periodic reviews. There is an important principle in management, 'Delegate but don't forget'. If you forget, then take it for granted that everyone else would have definitely forgotten. So, the principle of execution is to delegate but keep reviewing it periodically.

□

8

Grievance Management

When someone is going through a storm, your silent presence is more powerful than a million empty words.

—Thema Davis[12]

Management of grievances is an important aspect of temple management and for that matter of any institution. Broadly speaking, grievance means any real or imaginary feeling of dissatisfaction and injustice which a devotee has about the temple or that an employee has about his employment relationship. A well-defined grievance redressal procedure is an important element of a sound institution. Prompt and effective redressal of grievances is the key to industrial/institutional peace.

Features[13]

1. A grievance refers to any form of discontent or dissatisfaction relating to any aspect of organisation.
2. This dissatisfaction must arise out of engagement/ employment and not due to personal or family problems.
3. The dissatisfaction may be expressed or implied.
4. The dissatisfaction may be valid and legitimate or irrational or ridiculous or based on false reasons.

5. A grievance arises only when a devotee or an employee feels that injustice has been done to him.
6. Grievance, if not redressed in time, tends to lower the morale and productivity.

Causes/sources of grievances may be grouped under the following headings:

1. *Grievance arising out of working conditions:* Poor physical condition of workplace, very tight production standards, non-availability of proper tools and machines, unplanned changes in schedules and procedures, failure to maintain proper discipline, mismatch of workers with the job, poor relationship with the supervisor.
2. *Grievance arising out of management policy:* Wages and method of wage payment, overtime and incentive schemes, seniority, transfers; promotions, demotions and discharge; timings of the shift, lack of opportunities for career growth; penalties imposed for misconduct; leave; hostility towards trade union.
3. *Grievances arising out of alleged violation of:* The collective bargaining agreement, company rules and regulations; past practice; Central or state laws, responsibilities of management.
4. *Grievances arising out of personal maladjustment: Over-ambition; excessive self-esteem; impractical attitude to life.*

The following are the proactive methods of addressing grievances[14]:

1. *Exit Interview*

Information collected from the exiting employee on various aspects of working conditions forcing him to quit is supposed to be more credible than those expressed by the existing workers.

2. *Gripe-box System*

Devotees/employees may be encouraged to drop

anonymous complaints as they may fear that their identity may invite victimisation, especially when they complain against the management. This method is more appropriate when there is lack of trust and understanding between employees and their supervisors.

3. *Opinion Survey*

Various surveys, like morale survey, attitude survey, job satisfaction survey, grievance survey or comprehensive survey comprising all the above aspects, reveal vital inputs about the negative aspects of functioning of the organisation. Since the survey is conducted by persons other than the supervisor and the respondent's identity is not insisted upon, information collected is likely to be reliable.

4. *Meetings*

Group meetings, periodical interviews, collective bargaining sessions, informal get-togethers may be used to collect information about grievances.

5. *Open-door Policy*

Under this policy any employee can lodge a complaint or file his grievance with the manager designated for this purpose. The very objective of this policy is to encourage upward communication.

It is worth noting here that companies, like TELCO engage the family members of the employees in some projects, which help in creating a conducive and supportive family atmosphere.

At Shirdi

Online feedback: Devotee satisfaction was the item to be investigated at the Sai Baba Sansthan. I invited students and some employees to interview the devotees when they made their exit from the *Samadhi Mandir*. A feedback form was prepared with tick boxes for the interviewer. It was in the form of a Google spreadsheet and was available online. Some devotees gave their feedback through the forms in Google and some were interviewed physically. The devotees talked about the *darshan* experience, *ladoo prasad*, *udi prasad*, accommodation, Sansthan hospital, *prasad* food, donation counters, online booking, facilities at railway station and so on. Normally it was observed that the devotees were satisfied with the *darshan* that they just had and preferred not to complain. However, there were many who spoke openly and frankly. It was found that the overall satisfaction level was of the order of 80 per cent. However, there is a scope for improvement in all the processes and systems to increase the devotee satisfaction.

Get-together: I had organised a get-together of the relatives of the patients that were admitted to the Sansthan Hospitals. A public meeting was held in the hospital premises. The subject item was regarding the hospital services. People spoke openly about the shortfalls and also about the good things and good doctors. The reactions were mixed. I asked a number of questions from the audience regarding various issues related to the hospital. Right from the admission process, availability of medicine, food quality, doctor's visits, nursing to the discharge of the patient. People were asked to raise their hands if they agreed. It was observed that the overall satisfaction level regarding the hospital services was of the order of 90 per cent. People at the bottom of the pyramid are the patients of the hospitals at Shirdi. Based on the feedback then, we decided to make Sainath General Hospital totally free for all the patients. We also decided to provide free food and free accommodation to the relatives who had come to assist the patients. We also decided to provide bus fare to the patients at the time of discharge to return to their home. The patients at the Sansthan Hospitals come from the economically very poor category.

Morcha (Protests)

The level of satisfaction of the local residents varied from deeply satisfied to frustrated. There is a good amount of activism among the residents of Shirdi. Being locals, they enjoy some privileges in the temple *darshan*. A special gate and free entry to the *Samadhi Mandir* is given to the local residents. The current and erstwhile members of the Nagar Panchayat play a lead role among the residents. Many of them are co-operative, but not all of them have the same intent. It was observed that some residents had vested interests. They run the business of real estate and are interested in selling their lands to the temple. They try to overpower the Sansthan with agitations and *morchas* if their designs are not fulfilled. They buy land from the original landowners in lakhs and want the temple to purchase that land in crores. This was the exact nature of the situation. I refused to budge under pressure. Some of the aggrieved people staged a funeral procession (*antim yatra*) of my effigy and burned my effigy in the crematorium (*smashan*). Some attacked my car and caused serious damage. The then Chief Minister Hon'ble Devendra Fadnavis was quick to support me and ordered strict police action against the culprits. This was a very distressing situation for my family and me. While this was happening outside the Board meeting hall in Sai Nivas, I was busy in the meeting and my wife was watching this daylight drama from the Sai Nivas room. It became the breaking news on all news channels. Next day, almost all the TV channels arranged special discussions on this scenario. This uncouth incident had maligned the image of Shirdi. After strong police action in this matter, the Board meetings became peaceful, otherwise they were raising objections over some issue or the other.

Transparency

I was constantly vigilant to ensure that the temple working was kept transparent and free from any kind of corruption. I used to meet the vendors randomly, call them for meetings, organise vendors' meet, discuss with them one-to-one and listen to their grievances. Except for the accusation of corruption levelled by one vendor against one of the Trustees, not a single incident of corruption was noticed during the entire period of my tenure. The above-mentioned accusation was taken very seriously. I requested the Hon'ble Chief Minister to order an inquiry into the matter. He immediately ordered an inquiry led by the Divisional Commissioner of Nashik. The inquiry process took a few months but the allegation could not be proved.

In public life, it is necessary that for one to remain clean and be seen as clean and transparent. Grievance management is an important aspect of any organisation and is therefore, an important aspect of temple management. It works like a lubricant in a machine that smoothens the operation.

□

9

Budget, Accounts and Audit

The budget is not just a collection of numbers,
but an expression of our values and aspirations.

—Jack Lew[15]

Budget speaks of the vision and assessment of the business. Accounts is the only place where progress of an organisation is presented in actual numbers. Audit keeps an eye on the budget and accounts. The accounting practices are standardised and are required to be followed by every organisation. The health of the organisation is reflected in the accounts. If the accounts are maintained meticulously, the working of the organisation becomes smooth. Though audit, budget, taxation are all parts of accounts, here, I shall deal with them separately.

What is a Budget[16]?

A budget is an estimation of revenue and expenses over a specified future period of time and is usually compiled and re-evaluated on a periodic basis. Budgets can be made for a person, a group of people, a business, a government, or just about anything else that makes and spends money. Usually, it is made on an annual basis.

Understanding Budgeting

A budget is a microeconomic concept that shows the trade-off made when one good is exchanged for another. In terms of the bottom line–or the end result of this trade-off–a surplus budget means that profits are anticipated; a balanced budget means revenue are expected to equal the expenses; and a deficit budget means expenses will exceed revenue. To manage the monthly expenses, one has to prepare for life's unpredictable events, and be able to afford big-ticket items without landing into debt; so budgeting is important. Keeping track of how much one earns and spends means that one must know where the money goes and exercise greater control over his or her finances.

- A budget is an estimation of income and expenses over a specified future period of time and is utilised by governments, businesses and individuals.
- A budget is basically a financial plan for a defined period, normally a year, that is known to greatly enhance the success of any financial undertaking.
- Corporate budgets are essential for operating at peak efficiency.
- Aside from earmarking resources, a budget can also aid in setting goals, measuring outcomes and planning for contingencies.
- Personal budgets are extremely useful in managing an individual's or family's finances over both the short- and long-term horizon.

Corporate Budgets

Budgets are an integral part of running any business efficiently and effectively.

Budget Development Process

The process begins by establishing assumptions for the upcoming budget period. These assumptions are related to future sales trends, cost trends and the overall economic outlook of the market, industry or sector. Specific factors affecting potential expenses are addressed and monitored. The budget is published in a packet that outlines the standards and procedures used to develop it, including the assumptions about the markets, key relationships with vendors that provide discounts and explanations of how certain calculations were made.

The sales budget is often the first to be developed, as subsequent expense budgets cannot be established without knowing future cash flows. Budgets are developed for all the different subsidiaries, divisions and departments within an organisation. For a manufacturer, a separate budget is often developed for direct materials, labour and overhead.

All budgets get rolled up into the master budget, which also includes budgeted financial statements, forecasts of cash inflows and outflows and an overall financing plan. In a corporation, the top management reviews the budget and submits it for approval to the Board of Directors.

At the Sai Baba temple, the annual budget is prepared, presented and discussed in a Board meeting. It is of the order of around Rs.700/- crores. The various heads of accounts, perceived revenue and expenses are indicated in the budget for the forthcoming year. It has to be sent to the Maharashtra State Assembly for approval, along with the statement of accounts and balance sheet.

What is Accounting[17]?

Accounting is the process of recording financial transactions pertaining to a business. The accounting process includes summarising, analysing and reporting these transactions to oversight agencies, regulators and tax-collection entities. The financial statements used in accounting are a concise summary of financial transactions over an accounting period, summarising a company's operations, financial position and cash flows.

How Accounting Works

Accounting is one of the key functions for almost any

business. It may be handled by a bookkeeper or an accountant at a small firm, or by sizable finance departments with dozens of employees in larger companies. The reports generated by various streams of accounting, such as cost accounting and managerial accounting, are invaluable in helping management to make informed business decisions.

- Regardless of the scale of a business, accounting is a necessary function for decision-making, cost planning and measurement of economic performance.
- A bookkeeper can handle basic accounting needs, but a Certified Public Accountant (CPA) should be employed for larger or more advanced accounting tasks.
- Two important types of accounting systems for businesses are managerial accounting and cost accounting. Managerial accounting helps management teams make business decisions, while cost accounting helps business owners decide how much a product should cost.
- Professional accountants follow a set of standards known as the Generally Accepted Accounting Principles (GAAP) when preparing financial statements.

The financial statements that summarise a large company's operations, financial position and cash flows over a particular period are concise and consolidated reports based on thousands of individual financial transactions. As a result, all accounting designations are the culmination of years of study and rigorous examinations combined with a minimum number of years of practical accounting experience. There are various types of accounting as follows:

Financial Accounting

Financial accounting refers to the processes used to generate interim and annual financial statements. The results of all financial transactions that occur during an accounting period are summarised into the balance sheet, income statement and cash flow statement. The financial statements of most companies are audited annually by an external CA firm. For some, such as publicly traded companies, audits are a legal requirement. However, lenders also typically require the results of an external audit annually as part of their debt covenants. Therefore, most companies will have annual audits for one reason or another.

Managerial Accounting

Managerial accounting uses much of the same data as financial accounting, but it organises and utilises information in different ways; namely, in managerial accounting, an accountant generates monthly or quarterly reports that a business management team can use to make decisions about how the business operates. Managerial accounting also encompasses many other facets of accounting, including budgeting, forecasting and various financial analysis tools. Essentially, any information that may be useful to management falls underneath this umbrella. Normally MIS reports or monthly information statements are generated for the purpose of management reporting.

Cost Accounting

Just as managerial accounting helps businesses make decisions about management, cost accounting helps businesses make decisions about costing. Essentially, cost accounting considers all of the costs related to producing a product. Analysts, managers, business owners and accountants use this information to determine what their product should cost. In cost accounting, money is cast as an economic factor in production, whereas in financial accounting, money is considered as a measure of a company's economic performance.

Requirements for Accounting

In most cases, accountants use generally accepted

accounting principles (GAAP) when preparing financial statements. GAAP is a set of standards and principles designed to improve the comparability and consistency of financial reporting across industries. Its standards are based on double-entry accounting–a method in which every accounting transaction is entered as both a debit and credit in two separate general ledger accounts that will roll up into the balance sheet and income statement.

Example of Accounting

To illustrate double-entry accounting, imagine a business sends an invoice to one of its clients. An accountant using the double-entry method records a debit to accounts receivables, which flows through to the balance sheet and a credit to sales revenue, which flows through to the income statement. When the client pays the invoice, the accountant credits account receivables and debits cash. Double-entry accounting is also called balancing the books, as all of the accounting entries are balanced against each other. If the entries aren't balanced, the accountant knows there must be a mistake somewhere in the general ledger.

History of Accounting

The history of accounting has been around almost as long as money itself. Accounting history dates back to ancient civilisations of Mesopotamia, Egypt and Babylon. For example, during the Roman Empire, the government maintained detailed records of their finances. However, modern accounting as a profession has only been around since the early 19th century. Luca Pacioli is considered the 'Father of Accounting and Bookkeeping' due to his contribution to the development of accounting as a profession. An Italian mathematician and friend of Leonardo da Vinci, Pacioli published a book on the double-entry system of bookkeeping in 1494. By 1880, the modern profession of accounting was fully formed and recognised by the Institute of Chartered Accountants in England and Wales. This institute created many of the systems which accountants practice today. The formation of the institute occurred in large part due to the Industrial Revolution. Merchants not only needed to track their records, but sought to avoid bankruptcy as well.

Importance of Accounting for Investors

The work performed by accountants is at the heart of modern financial markets. Without accounting, investors would be unable to rely on timely or accurate financial information and companies' management would lack the transparency needed to manage risks or plan projects. Regulators also rely on accountants for critical functions, such as providing auditors opinions on companies. In short, although accounting is sometimes overlooked, it is absolutely critical for the smooth functioning of modern finance.

Audit[18]

Definition: Audit is the examination or inspection of various books of accounts by an auditor followed by physical checking of inventory to make sure that all departments are following a documented system of recording transactions. It is done to ascertain the accuracy of financial statements provided by the organisation.

Description: Audit can be done internally by employees or heads of a particular department known as internal audit and externally by an outside firm or an independent auditor, known as statutory audit. The idea is to check and verify the accounts by an independent authority to ensure that all books of accounts are done in a fair manner and there is no misrepresentation or fudging or fraud that is being conducted.

All the public listed firms have to get their accounts audited by an independent auditor before they declare their results for any quarter.

Who can Perform an Audit?

In India, chartered accountants from ICAI or the Institute of Chartered Accountants of India can conduct independent audits of any organisation. There are four main steps in the auditing process. The first one is to define the auditor's role and the terms of engagement which is usually in the form of a letter duly signed by the client. The second step is to plan the audit which would include details of deadlines and the departments the auditor would cover. Is it a single department or whole organisation which the auditor would be covering? The audit could last a day or even a week, depending upon the nature of the audit. The next important step is compiling the information from the audit. When an auditor audits the accounts or inspects key financial statements of a company, the findings are usually put out in a report or compiled in a systematic manner. The last and most important element of an audit is reporting the result. The results are documented in the auditor's report.

At Shirdi, there is an internal auditor who works at the Sansthan on a daily basis . He checks all the receipts and payments of the Sansthan. Then there is an external statutory auditor who audits the accounts independently and gives his report to the Sansthan.

Taxation[19]

The tax structure in India is divided into Direct and Indirect Taxes. While direct taxes are levied on taxable income earned by individuals and corporate entities, the burden to deposit taxes is on the assessees themselves. On the other hand, indirect taxes are levied on the sale and provision of goods and services respectively and the burden to collect and deposit taxes is on the sellers instead of the assessees directly.

The taxation system in India is such that the taxes are levied by the Central Government and the state governments. Some minor taxes are also levied by the local authorities, such as the municipality and the local governments.

Over the last few years, the Central and many state governments have undertaken various policy reforms and process simplification towards great predictability, fairness and automation. This has consequently led to India's meteoric rise to the top 100 in the World Bank's Ease of Doing Business (EoDB) ranking in 2019, as India jumped 79 positions from 142nd (2014) to 63rd (2019) in 'World Bank's Ease of Doing Business Ranking 2020'. The Goods and Services Tax (GST) reform is one such reform to ease the complex multiple indirect tax regime in India.

Tax Raids[20]

'Search and survey operations' are conducted by the Income Tax Department, also called raids, when they suspect an individual or business to have hoarded illegal money. A legal move against corruption by the Indian government! Time and again, the Indian government has taken initiatives to discourage hoarding of black money. Out of all the viable ways to curb illegal wealth, income tax raids have been the practice. Let's understand in detail about income tax raids and how to prevent them:

When does a Raid Happen?

An income tax raid, technically known as the process of search and seizure, is one of the crucial weapons that the Income Tax Department possesses to check black money. It is a measure that is known to be constitutionally valid too. A raid gets triggered under any of the following circumstances:

- Credible information of tax evasion; for instance, any evasion coming out of reports received from the intelligence wing of the Income Tax Department.
- Information coming from government departments.
- Information procured from assessment records of taxpayers.
- Information received with regard to spending being disproportionate to income of the taxpayer, i.e. an instance of lavish spending without corresponding income to match the same.
- Manipulation of books of accounts, vouchers, invoices, etc.

- Illegal investment in real estate.
- Unexplained cash credits, share transactions, etc.

How to Prevent a raid?

One can lawfully avoid a tax raid by being compliant in terms of responding to summons and notices sent to him by the department and also refrain from keeping money, property undeclared.

Thus, we understand that all the functions of accounting are important for managing a business. It is not just a one-man show, but teamwork. Department of Company Secretary and the official who deals with the Charity Commissioner should be informed to deal with the respective jobs.

Such is the importance of the accounts and related activities. All these aspects of accounts are valid and applicable to the temple. Therefore, temple management will be incomplete without budget, accounts and audits.

□

Section-3

Functional Management

10

Marketing Management

Leadership and learning are indispensable to each other.

—John F. Kennedy[3]

You may notice that temples offer various services and they also charge for these services in the temples. New services can be designed, keeping in mind the religion and public need. The result of all these efforts would be to increase the devotee satisfaction and earn revenue for the temple. Though it may smell like commercialisation of the temple, in reality it is not. We are serving to the needs of the devotees. We are only talking about the temple management using the terminology of marketing management. We have retained the term 'marketing management' as it is since it is a part of management. But when it comes to the temple, it should be read as service management and the temple provides services to the devotees.

Marketing Management[21]

Marketing management identifies market opportunities and comes out with appropriate strategies for exploring these opportunities profitably. It has to implement a marketing programme and evaluate continuously the effectiveness of marketing-mix. It has to remove the deficiencies observed in the actual execution of marketing plans, policies and procedures. It looks after the marketing system of the enterprise.

Management is the process of getting things done in an organised and efficient manner. Marketing management aims at efficient operation of marketing activities. Marketing management smoothens the process of exchange of ownership of goods and services from seller to the buyer. Marketing management, like all other areas of management, comprises the function of planning, organising, directing, coordinating and controlling.

At Shirdi

Aarti

The working of Shri Sai Baba temple at Shirdi starts from 4.00 a.m. and continues up to 10.30 p.m. Four *aartis*, vis. *kakad aarti* at 4.30 a.m., *madhyanha aarti* at 12.00 noon, *dhoop aarti* at sunset and *shej aarti* at 10.30 p.m. are performed every day. Devotees pay separate charges in order to attend the *aarti*. The charges for each *aarti* are different. Around 200 to 300 devotees can attend each of the *aartis*. It has to be booked online in advance. Normally there is a waiting period of around 15 days for attending the *aartis*.

Dress for Baba

A decorated dress is adorned on Baba before every *aarti* except for *kakad aarti*. The dress for the *shej aarti* is normally plain but in different colours. These colours are also pre-decided for all the days. It is yellow on Sunday, white on Monday, magenta on Tuesday, pink on Wednesday, orange on Thursday, green on Friday, blue on Saturday. The same dress is continued for the *kakad aarti*. Once the *kakad aarti* is over, a new dress is adorned in the morning after performing a holy bath. Any devotee can offer the dress for Baba. They can purchase it and hand it over to the Sansthan. There are a number of dress manufacturers in Shirdi. The dress costs in the range of Rs. 000/- to Rs. 40,000/-. There again is a waiting list for offering the dress for Baba. It can be booked online. The booking is not transferable.

VIP *Darshan*

Sai Baba temple in Shirdi has a system of VIP *darshan* pass. On payment of Rs. 200/- each, the devotee can avail quick *darshan* through a separate queue; the long queue can be avoided. This system was prevalent in the temple but the VIP *darshan* pass could be issued only to those who possess recommendation letters from MPs, MLAs or ministers. This had given rise to a large number of agents and even false recommendation letters. On my tour of the temple premises, I noticed that there was a rush at the PRO's office, where such VIP *darshan* passes were issued. Naturally, it was a crowd of agents. One fine morning, I decided to do away with the recommendation process. VIP passes were made available to everyone without any recommendation letter. Also, I allowed online booking for VIP *darshan*. The crowd at the PRO's office suddenly vanished. And in the first year, the revenue from such VIP passes had increased from Rs. 18 crores to Rs. 43 crores. In the second year, the revenue further increased to Rs. 61 crores. It means that, in the past, this much money was getting siphoned off by agents from the temple revenue.

Satyavrat Pooja

Sai *satyavrat pooja* is performed every day in the morning in the temple premises. It is similar to the well-known *satyanarayan pooja*. The scripture is different for this *pooja*. There is a pre-booking and a waiting list for the *pooja*. The charges include the items required for the *pooja*. It is guided by the temple *pujari*, normally called Guruji, and all the couples sitting in the *pooja* hall follow him.

Abhishek

Similar to the *satyavrat pooja, abhishek pooja* is performed every day in the temple premises. There is a separate scripture for performing the *pooja* and a separate hall where it is performed. Guruji leads the *pooja* and all the couples follow him. Here too, there is a pre-booking and a waiting list for the *pooja*.

Live *Darshan*

Live *darshan* of Sai Baba is telecast on Tata Sky TV, right from the opening of the temple till its closing. The transmission signal for live *darshan* is auctioned every year and whosoever offers the maximum amount gets the rights to transmit. Tata Sky pays an amount of Rs. 3.0 crores every year. Earlier the amount was meagre, but during my tenure, the auction was held for the first time and the amount received by the temple was multifold. The Sansthan has allowed Tata Sky to install their camera and transmitter in the *Samadhi Mandir*.

New Services

I can envision the following services for the temples. There could be more such services provided you are willing to stretch your imagination.

Car *Pooja*

There is a huge demand for *pooja* which is performed on buying a new car. The temple can deploy one of the *pujaris* for performing the *pooja* of the new cars. The buyer of the new car will get psychological satisfaction that his car is now safe for him and that Baba will take care of him.

Gruha Pooja

Similarly, when a new house is built or purchased, the *gruha shanti pooja* is performed by the buyer. If the temple can provide the *pujari* for performing this *pooja* on a chargeable basis, the buyer will get much satisfaction and the temple will receive revenue.

Weddings

If the temple can offer a wedding hall and the related infrastructure at a reasonable rate, there would be a large number of devotees who would prefer to get married at Shirdi.

This is prevalent in south India and also in some other parts of the country. This would be a great service to the society. At the same time, it may provide some earnings to the temple. It will generate employment for a large number of persons.

Birthdays

Nowadays, almost everyone celebrates his or her birthday; it has become a trend. If the temple facilitates the organisation of birthday celebrations in the temple premises along with a special *darshan* provided to them, it would be very much in demand. This also will provide satisfaction to a large number of devotees and generate employment and income.

Photograph with Deity

Devotees love to have their photograph clicked with the deity while taking *darshan*. An online system could be set up to click the photographs automatically at a pre-decided frequency. All such photographs can be uploaded on the temple website and the devotees can be allowed to download them on payment basis at specially-installed terminals. If a temple does not do this, the shop owners and photographers outside the temple premises will do it and earn their livelihood. This could be done through an app which will enable the devotee to download his/her photo from the Net using mobile.

Marketing management is one of the important aspects of temple management. It is a pure service model for the temple. Ultimately, the temple is a holy service to the devotees. By providing better service, the temple can earn revenue and can also give satisfaction to the devotees visiting the temple. What is the takeaway message from marketing management? That the temple gives intangible things and gets tangible returns. But these intangibles are valuable for the devotee's satisfaction.

Let me narrate a small observation here to explain my point of view. Once, I visited a famous temple in Gujarat, viz. Dwarkadhish temple in Dwarka. It is known as one of the four *dhams* or *char dham*, the other three being Jagannath

Puri, Rameshwaram and Badrinath. There were a number of *gwalas* (cowherds) with their cows standing in a row. They had brought grass with them. The scheme was that devotees would buy the grass from them and feed their cow and in return will earn *punya*. This is servicing the devotees' needs. This is exactly the scheme in all the temples that you give in tangible form and what you get in return is more valuable but in intangible form. Thus, marketing is nothing but service to the devotees and an important aspect of temple management in order to increase the devotee's satisfaction and also the revenue of the temple.

□

11

Purchase Management

The harder you work for something,
the greater you'll feel when you achieve it.

—Unknown[22]

What is purchase management[23]?

Purchase management is a business discipline that enables companies to manage the activities and relationships that make up the purchasing functions necessary to do business. At its core, purchase management is all about saving money, increasing profits and it is an important function for any wholesale, distribution or manufacturing business.

Efficient purchase management provides a prime opportunity to wholesalers to clear bigger profits by controlling costs of the inventory stock needed to run their business. To deliver the greatest profitability for an organisation, it is crucial that products and services are purchased at the best price, just in time and of the best quality available.

To ensure the most cost-effective outcomes, purchasing strategies are necessary and should be developed in line with a basic purchasing cycle to best manage all the necessary functions from one centralised location.

Purchasing Cycles

A purchasing cycle shows the steps that a business will go through before making any product purchase. It starts from the knowledge that there is a product need, to specifying the quantities required and when they are needed. Once a purchase need is identified, the prices and quality of different products and inventory stock from different suppliers need to be compared before a decision is reached on where to source the goods. A purchase order is then approved; in larger organisations this may require approval from more than one person.

The business and the supplier then negotiate the terms of the purchase contract. At this stage of the purchasing cycle, it may also be determined if this is a one-off sale or whether it will be an ongoing relationship with the chosen supplier. When the stock is receipted into the business, the goods are counted and inspected for quality and then recorded in the company's inventory management system.

Why Purchase Management Matters?

Purchase management impacts cash flow, inventory stock costs, contractual issues and product availability. Therefore, it is crucial for businesses to have a good process for procuring their inventory stock. The most basic principle of purchase management is that goods and services must always be purchased and delivered at the best possible price to help maximise profits. Excess inventory stock costs money to hold and it represents an opportunity cost when the money could have been better spent elsewhere.

Purchase management matters because the process of acquiring the right goods, for the right price and at the right time, matters. If we are paying too much for the stock required in retail or manufacturing business, it can seriously reduce our profits.

Benefits of Purchase Management

Purchase management is a system that creates customised

approval rules providing the ability to hasten approvals and order placement for the timely receipt of inventory stock.

Purchase management streamlines the purchasing and inventory control process of an organisation for greater efficiency and lower costs.

Purchase Management Solutions

Implementing software into warehouse operations optimises the management and control of purchasing inventory stock across multiple channels or for a single location. The systems improve inventory control and help create better supplier relationships because everything is tracked from one centralised location. Purchasing operations integrate and electronically connect the organisation to real-time inventory stock data.

At Shirdi

At Sai Baba Sansthan, Shirdi, the purchase of all the goods and services is done as per the procedure laid down by the government of Maharashtra. All purchases above Rs. 3.0 lakhs are to be made through the process of e-tendering using the portals of the government of Maharashtra. It starts with the preparation of estimates and detailed specifications of the purchase items. Once the item is approved in the meeting of the Board of Trustees, the respective departments take the initiative to process the item for purchase. The first step is to publish the tender notice in newspapers and on the Sansthan's website. The government has approved guidelines regarding the advertisement. The level of publicity is proportionate to the cost of the tender. The proportion of advertisement in local-, state-level and national-level newspapers is defined in the guidelines. The tender notice has a specifically designed format. It should contain the schedule of dates for opening and closing of the tender, the date of pre-bid meeting if any, cost of tender document, earnest money deposit, etc. Some details of the procedure are given in Appendix-2.

Two-envelope System

Normally, two-envelope systems are followed. First envelope contains the technical bid and the second one contains the financial bid. The vendors have to upload their offers online on the portal and also have to submit them physically. If the vendor is found eligible as per the technical bid, only then does he become eligible to compete further. The financial bid is then opened on the portal for all those who are eligible and the offer of the lowest vendor, also called as L-1, is accepted. If there are two vendors who are at L-1 position, the order is divided between those two vendors. If the L-1 refuses to comply, then the offer goes to L-2 and so on. The tenders are opened on the portal in the presence of all the vendors.

Purchase Order

The purchase order is placed with the successful vendor and he is then asked to provide the goods or services as per the specifications. Purchase order is a legal document and hence should be finalised in consultation with the legal department. On delivery, the goods are inspected and only if found as per the intent, they are accepted and the vendor is paid accordingly. If the material is not as per the specifications, then it is rejected. The supplier is given one chance to rectify the supplies. Otherwise, the work order is cancelled and the vendor is blacklisted.

The above process is fully transparent and is without human intervention. The annual purchase at Sai Sansthan is around Rs. 300 crores. Just to cite an example, the temple requires to annually purchase *ghee* costing around Rs. 35 crores, vegetables and grocery items around Rs. 100 crores and so on. Efficient purchase management is a crucial part of the temple management.

□

12

Contracts Management

The true measure of the value of any business leader and manager is performance.

—Brian Tracy[3]

The works of any organisation are to be executed through contracts. There shall be a duly authorised process of awarding the contract. All the steps of estimation, specification, tender documentation, tender notice, pre-bid meeting, opening of tenders and awarding the contract are to be systematically followed as explained in detail in the earlier chapter on purchase.

Contract Management[24]

Contract management is the process of managing contracts, deliverables, deadlines, contract terms and conditions while ensuring customer satisfaction. Public and private organisations know that purchasing does not end when the contract is awarded. Effective post-award contract management is essential.

Contract Manager

Each day is a different challenge for contract managers. Every great project starts with a contract. It takes a qualified professional to be detail-oriented, collaborative and committed to action. Successful contract managers are able to:

- Write, analyse and respond to proposals
- Negotiate price, terms and conditions
- Manage the contract throughout the process
- Identify risks and solve problems as they arise
- Advocate for and monitor compliance
- Maintain records of existing and past contracts

How Contract Management Works

1. *Managing service delivery*: This ensures that products are delivered as and when they are ordered.
2. *Managing the relationship*: Involves strengthening the contact between vendor and purchaser to allow for improved communication throughout the process of contract management.
3. *Managing the contract*: The ongoing administration that ensures the day-to-day procurement activities follows what is detailed in the agreement
4. *Seeking improvements*: Amendments and alterations are pursued within a procurement environment in order to improve efficiencies and generate an increase in profits.
5. *Ongoing assessment*: Procurement activities are assessed continuously to ensure that contracts are honoured and all purchasing processes have been followed.
6. *Managing change*: As part of a long-term procurement relationship, the changes in activities, requirements or products need to be noted and handled effectively.
7. *Managing renewal or termination*: When a contract is due for renewal, it is necessary to decide on taking proactive steps to understand whether the contracts should be renewed as is, re-negotiated or terminated, based on future business needs, commercial attractiveness and previous performance by the supplier.

At Shirdi

There is a separate contract department at Sai Sansthan, Shirdi to manage all the works through the system of e-tendering. Purchase is comparatively a short-term activity. However, the contract of a civil, electrical, mechanical work, wherein *in-situ* construction activities get involved, is time-consuming and hence, a long-term activity. The payment made to the contractor is in steps and is related to the progress of work at the site. It should be remembered that the payment schedule is the most important part of the work contract. At no point of time, should the contractor be paid more than what he has spent on the works. If he is overpaid, there is a possibility that the contractor may leave the job halfway through. Then it becomes difficult to wind up the ongoing contract and award the job to another contractor. If the matter goes in litigation, it may linger for years. Some details of the contract procedure are given in Appendix-3.

Incentive and Penalty

Once I met Hon'ble Shri Nitin Gadkari (currently Union Minister for Highways, Road Transport) when he was Minister for Public Works in Maharashtra. He had constructed 50 over-bridges and the Pune-Mumbai Expressway within five years in the city of Mumbai, during his tenure. While revealing the secret of speedy construction, he said: "I have included two clauses in the contract agreement. One, the contractor will be given an incentive if he completes the contract ahead of schedule and have specified the amount of incentive. Second, the contractor will be penalised if he delays the contract beyond the schedule and the amount of penalty is specified. His experience was that almost everyone performed well and completed the contracted works ahead of schedule. Therefore, the clauses of incentive and penalty are helpful in the execution of the contract.

Contract agreement or work order is a legal document. One must specifically bear in mind that if the contractor fails and there arises the need to terminate him, then there shall be proper clauses included in the contract agreement. Normally, in case of a dispute, the matter is sent to the arbitrator. One of the terms of the contract could be that the CEO of the owning organisation shall be the sole arbitrator and that his decision shall be final and binding on both the parties. Though, nobody can stop the contractor from approaching the court of law, this clause will be helpful for the owners.

Thus, contract management is an important activity of temple management. It should be remembered that a work order or a contract agreement is a legal document. Therefore, the legal department/lawyer should be roped in before execution of such contracts.

□

13

Financial Management

Finance is not merely about making money.
It's about achieving our deep goals
and protecting the fruits of our labor.
It's about stewardship and,
therefore, about achieving a good society.

—Robert J. Shiller[25]

Financial management provides pathways to attain goals and objectives in an organisation. Organisational efficiency can be measured through proper allocation, acquisition and management of funds.

Meaning of Financial Management[26]

Financial management means planning, organising, directing and controlling the financial activities, such as procurement and utilisation of funds of the enterprise. This means applying general management principles to financial resources of the enterprise.

Scope/Elements

1. Investment decisions include investment in fixed assets (called 'capital budgeting'). Investment in current assets is also a part of investment decisions, called 'working capital' decisions.

2. Financial decisions relate to the raising of finance from various resources which will depend upon decision on type of source, period of financing, cost of financing and the returns thereby.
3. Dividend decision has to be taken by the finance manager, especially with regards to the net profit distribution. Net profits are generally divided into two:
    1. *Dividend for shareholders*: Dividend and the rate of it has to be decided.
    2. *Retained profits*: Amount of retained profits has to be finalised which will depend upon expansion and diversification plans of the enterprise.

Objectives of Financial Management

Financial management is generally concerned with procurement, allocation and control of financial resources of a concern. The objectives can be:

1. To ensure regular and adequate supply of funds to the concern.
2. To ensure adequate returns to the shareholders and this will depend upon the earning capacity, market price of the share and expectations of the shareholders.
3. To ensure optimum funds utilisation after the funds have been procured, is to utilise them in the maximum possible way at least cost.
4. To ensure safety of investment, i.e., funds should be invested in safe ventures so that adequate rate of return can be achieved.
5. To plan a sound capital structure, there should be a sound and fair composition of capital so that a balance is maintained between debt and equity capital.

Functions of Financial Management

1. ***Estimation of capital requirements:*** The finance manager has to make an estimate with regards to

capital requirements of the company/trust. This will depend upon expected costs and profits and future programmes and policies of the company. Estimations have to be made in an adequate manner so that the earning capacity of the enterprise increases.

2. ***Determination of capital composition:*** Once the estimate has been made, the capital structure has to be decided. This involves short-term and long-term debt equity analysis. This will depend upon the proportion of equity capital a company possesses and additional funds which have to be raised from outside parties.
3. ***Choice of sources of funds:*** For additional funds to be procured, a company has many choices, like:
    1. Issue of shares and debentures.
    2. Loans to be taken from banks and financial institutions.
    3. Public deposits to be drawn in the form of bonds.
4. ***Choice of factor*** will depend on relative merits and demerits of each source and period of financing.
5. ***Investment of funds:*** The finance manager has to decide to allocate funds in profitable ventures so that there is safety on investment and regular returns are possible.
6. ***Disposal of surplus:*** The net profits decision has to be made by the finance manager. This can be done in two ways:
    1. *Dividend declaration*: This includes identifying the rate of dividends and other benefits, like bonus.
    2. *Retained profits*: The volume has to be decided and this will depend upon expansional, innovative and diversification plans of the company.
7. ***Management of cash:*** the finance manager has to make decisions with regards to cash management. Cash is required for many purposes, like payment of wages and salaries, payment of electricity and water

bills, payment to creditors, meeting current liabilities, maintenance of enough stock, purchase of raw materials, etc. Nowadays cash has been almost done away with since digital payment has become possible.

8. ***Financial controls:*** The finance manager has not only to plan, procure and utilise the funds but he also has to exercise control over the finances. This can be done through many techniques, like ratio analysis, financial forecasting, cost and profit control, etc.

At Shirdi

Income and Expense

Similar to a business, a temple also needs to make the assessment of daily receipts and payments. As a mode of transparency, I had decided that the daily donation receipts should be displayed on the notice-board for the information of the public. At Shri Sai Baba temple in Shirdi, daily donation receipt through various modes is to the tune of Rs. 1.0 crores and another Rs. 1.0 crore from various other sources. Thus, the annual budget is of the order of around Rs. 700 crores.

Surpluses

The difference in receipts over payments is the profit of any organisation; here it is surplus. At Shirdi, the modes of expenses are for running two hospitals, five educational institutions, mega kitchen or *prasadalaya*, *Samadhi Mandir*, accommodations, transport and so on. Though it is mandatory to spend 85 per cent of the receipts, in the same year, towards the objectives of the Trust, clumsy procedures and local activism make this expenditure impossible. Hardly 50 per cent of the receipts can be spent. Therefore, the unspent amount is liable to become taxable in the hands of the Trust. Alternatively, development projects should be taken up and implemented by the Sansthan every year. This would save the taxes and provide good infrastructure for the benefit of the devotees.

Planning Finances

As stated above, the management of unspent amounts or the surplus amount becomes very important. It is advisable to utilise it for development work and for capital projects. These could be development of infrastructure, facilities for devotees, tourism development and so on. This is the only way that it can be spent. Financial planning of the Trust funds is very important from the point of view of achieving planned development.

Counting of Donations

There has to be a proper and transparent procedure for the counting of donations. At Sai Baba Sansthan, Shirdi, there are 52 donation-boxes placed in the temple premises. There is a well-defined and standardised process in place, for counting. It is described in detail in a separate chapter.

Banking and Bank Rating

All the receipts of the institution are to be deposited in the bank. Now when talking of banking, one needs to know the reputation and credibility of the bank. Banks are ranked according to their performance and their financial strength by the Reserve Bank of India. Generally, all the co-operative banks are rated as poor, with some exceptions. As of July 2020, after the recent mergers of government banks, there are a total of 12 nationalised banks in India and RBI is the governing body. All these banks have different business volumes and different financial ratings. The State Bank of India is the biggest with a volume of Rs. 46 lakh crores as their business volume.

Fixed Deposits

We are required to invest the unspent money to generate returns. It could be invested in shares, mutual funds, lands and properties or kept in the bank in the form of fixed deposits. Higher the returns offered on investment, higher will be the risk. Among all these investiments, shares are at higher risk, though opinions on this differ. Fixed deposits are comparatively safe and offer pre-decided returns. Plus, the liquidity of money invested in fixed deposits is highest. Here also, different banks offer different rates of interest. The lower the rating of the bank, the higher is the rate of interest offered by them. At Sai Baba Sansthan, Shirdi, the government of Maharashtra has made it mandatory to invest in fixed deposits with the nationalised banks only. So, there are 12 nationalised banks in Shirdi which are the investment bankers for the Sansthan. When the fixed deposits are to be created, all these banks are invited to offer competitive rates and the bank that offers the maximum rate on that day, receives the fixed deposits. Sansthan has fixed deposits of around Rs. 2,500 crores, but they cannot be kept in one bank. A proper combination of safe financial rating and rate of interest has to be worked out.

Thus, it would be noticed that the financial management of receipts and payments is a very important aspect of temple management. All the decisions in this regard are taken in the meetings of the Board of Trustees.

□

14

Water Management

Anyone who can solve the problems of water will be worthy of two Nobel prizes–one for peace and one for science.

—John F. Kennedy[27]

Water Management[28]

Water management is the management of water resources for the coming generations. Water is one the most crucial natural resources for the existence of human beings. In India, out of the total groundwater availability, only 6 per cent is used for domestic purposes and another 5 per cent for industrial purposes, while the remaining 89 per cent is used for agriculture.

Meaning of Water Management

Water resource management is the activity of planning, developing, distributing and making the optimum use of water resources. It is a subset of water cycle management. The water cycle, through evaporation and precipitation, maintains hydrological systems which form rivers and lakes and support a variety of aquatic ecosystems. Wetlands are intermediate forms between terrestrial and aquatic ecosystems and contain species of plants and animals that are highly moisture-dependent.

Statistics on Water

Water covers 70 per cent of the earth's surface but only 3 per cent of this is fresh water. Of this, 2 per cent is in polar ice caps and only 1 per cent is usable water in rivers, lakes and subsoil aquifers. Only a fraction of this can be actually used.

At a global level, 70 per cent of water is used for agriculture, about 25 per cent for industry and only 6 per cent for domestic use. However, this varies in different countries and industrialised countries use a greater percentage in industry. *India uses 89 per cent for agriculture, 5 per cent for industry and 6 per cent for domestic use. The total annual freshwater withdrawals today are estimated at 3800 cubic kilometres, twice as much as just 50 years ago (World Commission on Dams, 2000).*

Studies indicate that a person needs a minimum of 20 to 40 litres of water per day for drinking and sanitation. More than one billion people worldwide have no access to clean water. India is expected to face critical levels of water stress by 2025. At the global level, 31 countries are already short of water and by 2025, there will be 48 countries facing serious water shortages.

The UN has estimated that by the year 2050, 4 billion people will be seriously affected by water shortage. This will lead to multiple conflicts between countries over the sharing of water.

Around 20 major cities in India face chronic or interrupted water shortages. There are 100 countries that share the waters of 13 large rivers and lakes. International accords that will look at a fair distribution of water in such areas will become critical to world peace. India and Bangladesh already have a negotiated agreement on the water use of the Ganges.

Saving Water

Water harvesting: The technique to save water is called water harvesting. It can be done by two major processes:

1. ***Rainwater harvesting:*** It is a method of collection and

storage of rain-water into natural tanks or reservoirs. This stored water can be reused in the future.

2. ***Groundwater harvesting:*** Groundwater harvesting is a method to save water placed under the ground.
3. ***Drip irrigation:*** In this method, irrigation is done through dripping water slowly to the roots of various crops, either on to the soil surface or directly on to the root.
4. ***Water saving habits:*** There are various wise habits to conserve water. Like fixing leaky taps, lesser use of water during washing clothes, taking a quick shower instead of long baths.

Sustainable Water Management

'Save water' campaigns are essential to make people everywhere aware of the dangers of water scarcity. A number of measures need to be taken for better management of the world's water resources. These include measures such as:

- Building several small reservoirs instead of a few mega projects.
- Develop small catchment dams and protect wetlands.
- Soil management, micro catchment development and afforestation permit recharging of underground aquifers, thus reducing the need for large dams.
- Treating and recycling municipal wastewater for agricultural use.
- Preventing leakages from dams and canals.
- Preventing loss in municipal pipes.
- Effective rain-water harvesting in urban environments.
- Water conservation measures in agriculture, such as using drip irrigation.
- Pricing water at its real value makes people use it more responsibly and efficiently and reduces water wastage.
- In deforested areas, where land has been degraded,

soil management by bunding along the hill slopes and making '*nala*' plugs can help retain moisture and make it possible to revegetate degraded areas.

Dams Problems

- Fragmentation and physical transformation of rivers.
- Serious impacts on riverine ecosystems.
- Social consequences of large dams due to displacement of people.
- Waterlogging and salinisation of surrounding lands.
- Dislodging animal populations, damaging their habitat and cutting off their migration routes.
- Fishing and travel by boat disrupted.
- The emission of greenhouse gases from reservoirs due to rotting vegetation and carbon inflows from the catchment which is a recently-identified impact.

Kulhs in Himachal Pradesh

Parts of Himachal Pradesh have evolved a local system of canal irrigation, called *kulhs* over 400 years ago. The water flowing in the streams was diverted into man-made channels which took this water to numerous villages down the hillside. The management of water flowing in these kulhs was by common agreement among all the villages. Interestingly, during the planting season, water was first used by the village farthest away from the source of the *kulh*, then by villages progressively higher up. These *kulhs* were managed by two or three people who were paid by the villagers. In addition to irrigation, water from these *kulhs* also percolated into the soil and fed springs at various points.

Water-harvesting is an age-old concept in India. They are called as:

- *Khadins*, tanks and *nadis* in Rajasthan.
- *Bandharas* and *tals* in Maharashtra.
- *Bundhis* in Madhya Pradesh and Uttar Pradesh.
- *Ahars* and *pynes* in Bihar.
- *Kulhs* in Himachal Pradesh.

- Ponds in the Kandi belt of Jammu region.
- *Eris* (tanks) in Tamil Nadu.
- *Surangams* in Kerala.
- *Kattas* in Karnataka.

These are some of the ancient water-harvesting and water-conveyance structures still in use today. Water-harvesting techniques are highly locale-specific and the benefits are also localised. Giving people control over their local water resources ensures that mismanagement and over-exploitation of these resources is controlled.

So, water management is the need of the hour to save water for our future generations.

Water in Shirdi

Shri Sai Baba Sansthan, Shirdi gets water supply once in 30 to 60 days through the right water canal of Godavari from the Nashik Irrigation Department. It takes around 48 hours to fill up all the reservoirs. This water is sufficient for the entire temple facilities for around 45 to 60 days. Sansthan has four water reservoirs located in Kankuri village of Rahata *taluka* with the storage capacity of 164, 87, 18 and 42 million litres each, totalling about 311 million litres. During my tenure, the fourth water reservoir was built and the third one was commissioned. The water used in all the accommodations, *prasadalaya*, hospitals, schools, residential quarters, etc. is of the order of 4.0 to 4.5 million litres per day. In addition to this, Sansthan has eight wells and 13 borewells of its own as a source of water. This water is normally used for housekeeping, cleaning and gardening purposes.

Water Purification, Rain-water Harvesting, STP at Shirdi

Sansthan has its own water purification facility. In order to supply clean and purified water, Sansthan makes proper use of bleaching powder, alum and chlorine gas. The water is regularly tested in the government laboratories. Rain-water harvesting systems have been installed in all the existing buildings of the Sansthan. Sewage treatment plants (STP) also have been installed and the water so treated is used for flushing purposes and in the gardens.

There was a time when the Sansthan had to depend on the tanker-water supply in the months of April and May. At times, the tankers could not provide sufficient quantity of water and the lodging facilities at the Sansthan had to be closed. But now, with the increased capacity of water reservoirs and recycling of water, supply of water via tankers is no longer required. Thus, Shirdi is no longer dependent on water tankers. Water management is therefore an important part of temple management.

□

15

Waste Management

Solid wastes are the discarded leftovers of our advanced consumer society. This growing mountain of garbage and trash represents not only an attitude of indifference toward valuable natural resources, but also a serious economic and public health problem.

—Jimmy Carter[29]

Shirdi has Become a Clean Town[30]

The irony in India is that the more popular the place of pilgrimage, the more unclean is the town where it is located. I resolved to change this perception about Shirdi. We undertook a campaign–a collaboration between the Sansthan and the local Municipal Council, which responded positively. Residents also participated. Within a few days, Shirdi became a clean town.

After taking charge as chairman of Shri Sai Baba Sansthan, Shirdi, I focused my attention on transforming Shirdi into a clean and green town. It became a top priority on my agenda. I put forth a proposal regarding this in the meeting of the Board of Trustees. I had met with the Hon'ble President of India and the Hon'ble Prime Minister of India when I invited them to attend Sai Baba's Samadhi Centenary celebrations. Both were very keen on promoting public cleanliness. The then Chief

Minister of Maharashtra, Shri Devendra Fadnavis suggested that the Sansthan play a leading role and also bear the cost of the clean-up of Shirdi. So, we resolved that the Sansthan would take up the responsibility for the cleanliness of Shirdi. We resolved to provide funds of Rs. 42 lakhs (Rs.4.2 million) per month to the Municipal Council for the cleanliness drive.

Background

On the birth anniversary of Mahatma Gandhi, with the help of Sansthan employees, municipal employees, devotees, students and citizens decided to volunteer (*shramadaan*) to clean up Shirdi. When we realised that the major challenge was where to deposit the solid waste collected during the clean-up drive, the programme was postponed. There were six dried-up wells where people used to dump garbage. By this time, all of them were filled to the brim. I realised that there was an urgent need to find an alternative solution. I started to look for technological solutions to this problem.

Waste to Wealth

I wanted to carry out solid waste management, using the latest technology. From day one, I believed that solid waste is not a burden on society but a potential source of income. I wanted to prove that if the waste is viewed from an economic, technological or business point of view, it can definitely be a source of wealth.

This is a challenge for all scientists and technical experts. While approaching the issue of solid waste management, I divided the problem into four parts: 1) door-to-door collection of solid waste combined with segregation of dry and wet garbage, 2) transporting it to the processing centre, 3) using the latest technology to process solid waste at the centre and lastly 4) encashing on the products generated in the process, namely the fertiliser, gas and electricity produced.

Since the first two processes relate to administrative and government management, I shall refrain from commenting on them. The third part is something that interests all technologists. but all technologists must keep in mind that a technology is useful only if it is financially viable; else it becomes a mere showpiece. LED lights are widely used these days because they are affordable even for the common masses, else they would have remained decorative items. I consulted many people in this regard. Many experts were asked to make presentations on possible solutions during the meetings of the Board of Trustees. I visited solid waste processing plants at Goa, Solapur, Varanasi, Mumbai and many other cities and states. I also studied the scenario in some foreign countries, such as Sweden.

Different Methods

For the past few years, I have been studying the issue of solid waste management. Solid waste has become a critical issue in many big cities. This problem is compounded when it comes to towns that are places of pilgrimage and attract huge crowds. We often observe that while the temples themselves are clean, the surrounding town is quite dirty. I am a nuclear scientist and have worked as senior scientist in the Department of Atomic Energy, Government of India, for 27 years in the field of nuclear engineering. I approached this problem from a scientific perspective.

There are different ways of processing solid waste: 1) people gather the waste into small piles and then burn it; this is known as incineration; 2) people segregate the plastic waste and use it to generate fuel; 3) the waste can be fermented through use of bio-organic methods to produce fertilisers and gas. The gas can be used in the kitchen or to generate electricity. While this is scientifically possible, I found that it was not sufficient. I wanted the solution to be economically viable as well. Through my study visits, I realised that sufficiently advanced technology is available, but with only that alone, all the problems cannot be solved.

Solid Waste

Let us try to define solid waste–any waste can be defined

as 'a left over, a redundant product or material of no or marginal value for the owner and which the owner wants to discard'[22]. And solid waste is waste in solid state. Here we are mainly talking about city or residential waste only. We are not considering liquid or gaseous waste or clinical, pharmaceutical, electronic or hazardous solid waste.

A number of steps are involved in solid waste management (SWM), right from collecting, segregating, processing to the disposal of waste. The first step of collecting the waste, though very important, is not discussed here as it is more administrative than scientific in nature. But the economics and corruption involved in this step can overshadow the entire process. For example, how much waste is generated in Mumbai every day? At present the figure is 7,000 tonnes. Now the question is, who measured this and how? This has no answer. It is mostly done by the contracting firms who collect and dump it in the yard. The higher the number they show, the more they earn. In the case of Mumbai, the expenses for gathering and processing solid waste are beyond imagination. One authentic source told me that the contract for collecting solid waste and transporting it to the dumping ground is worth a whopping Rs.1,800 crores (Rs.18 billion). It is a fact that Brihanmumbai Municipal Corporation spends on tackling this issue, but the real question is what these funds are actually spent on? A major part of the expenditure is on transporting solid waste and dumping it, rather than on further processing it. Anyway, we are limiting ourselves to the technological part. Let us understand various technological methods available to treat the solid waste.

Technology

A number of established and alternative technologies are available to treat solid waste. Some of them are listed below:

1. Autoclaving
2. Fluffing
3. Melting

4. Incineration
5. Vermicomposting
6. Energy recovery
7. Thermal conversion
8. Advanced thermal treatment
9. Plasma gasification and plasma pyrolysis
10. Refuse-derived fuel
11. Fluidised bed technology
12. Bio-conversion
13. Dry anaerobic composting

Waste Import

Researchers are working on different methods of processing solid waste. Their concepts and goals differ widely. What they have in common, however, is the desire to work for the benefit of society. Mumbai generates 7,000 tonnes of solid waste daily. The disposal of this waste becomes a serious challenge as a huge space is required for dumping. How long the dumping ground can be used and how to manage the piles of solid waste–all these are challenges. If technology is not used to process solid waste, the number of dumping grounds would keep on increasing. Finding a solution is difficult but not impossible if technologists can apply their mind to this problem. Solid waste disposal has become a big business and there are even garbage mafia in existence.

It is not easy to tackle the problem of solid waste disposal. However, advanced technology is available today as scientists come up with new inventions. All that is required is political and administrative will power. I firmly believe that all the solid waste in the country can be converted into wealth. The day we accomplish this will be the day that India truly becomes Swachh Bharat. Not only will we have a cleaner environment, but the expenditure on healthcare can also reduce tremendously. In addition, this solid waste can be used to generate fertiliser, gas and electricity.

Some days ago, I was reading the history of Sweden. This

is the only nation in the world to process its entire solid waste output. The solid waste is used to generate different resources. *The Hindu* reported in its issue dated 12th December 2016 that Sweden had run out of garbage and had to import it from neighbouring countries. They realised that they were not getting sufficient solid waste to run their processing plants at full capacity, to produce power–they actually needed more solid waste to process. They even started to import solid waste from neighbouring countries, such as Norway, Denmark and Scotland. From the technological, scientific and economic perspective, waste is nothing but wealth. Sweden has proved that waste is not a liability.

Plant in Shirdi

Around 20 tonnes of solid waste is generated in Shirdi daily. Around 12 to 13 tonnes of garbage is generated in the town, including that of the hotels and seven to eight tonnes by the Sansthan activities. I have resolved to set up a waste processing plant with the capacity to process 20 tonnes of waste daily. This plant will be set up by the Sai Baba Sansthan. All the waste generated in the town and by the temple will be processed in this plant. I am confident that this project will make Shirdi truly a clean town.

All the technical formalities have been completed and this project will be underway in the near future. This project in Shirdi will become a model project for small towns. The various technologies available are listed above. I have narrowed down to the technological method of anaerobic bio-digestion that will be used to treat the solid waste in the plant. The gas generated through this project will be used for cooking, and the fertilisers generated will be utilised for farming or gardening. Since the project is small, it is not advisable to go for production of electricity. We have also worked out the financial viability of the project. Initially the plant will have the capacity to treat 10 tonnes of waste. The project will incur an initial cost of around Rs. 5 crores (Rs.50 million). This investment can be recovered within five years through the sale of fertilisers and use of the generated gas. After five years, the project will become profitable. Seven acres of land near the Sansthan's helipad at Shirdi have been identified for the location of the plant.

Anaerobic Bio-digestion

Anaerobic bio-digestion is a series of biological processes in which microorganisms break down biodegradable material in the absence of oxygen. One of the end products is biogas, which is combusted to generate electricity and heat or can be processed into renewable natural gas and transportation fuels. A range of anaerobic digestion technologies are converting livestock manure, municipal wastewater solids, food waste, high-strength industrial wastewater and residuals, fats, oils and grease (FOG) and various other organic waste streams into biogas, 24 hours a day, seven days a week. Separated digested solids can be composted, utilised for dairy bedding, directly applied to cropland or converted into other products. Nutrients in the liquid stream are used in agriculture as fertilisers.

The Biological Process

The digestion process begins with bacterial hydrolysis of the input materials to break down insoluble organic polymers, such as carbohydrates and make them available for the bacteria. Acidogenic bacteria then convert the sugars and amino acids into carbon dioxide, hydrogen, ammonia and organic acid, along with additional ammonia, hydrogen and carbon dioxide. Finally, methanogens convert these products to methane and carbon dioxide[24].

The plant is yet to be installed. Due to the Sansthan's efforts, Shirdi has been ranked as the second cleanest town in Maharashtra and the third cleanest town at the national level during Swachh Bharat Abhiyan. With everyone's cooperation, I was confident that Shirdi would become a clean and beautiful city. With the installation of the SWM plant, Shirdi will surely become the number one clean city in the country. I was filled with pride while felicitating the then Mayor of Shirdi, Mrs. Yogita Shelke (also a Trustee of the Sansthan). The felicitation was on the occasion of the Shirdi Municipal Council winning an award of Rs. 15 crores (Rs. 150 million) and being ranked third in India and second in Maharashtra for cleanliness as per the Swachh Bharat campaign survey of 2018 and 2019.

Biogas Plant

Shirdi is always crowded with visiting devotees, who come from all over India and from other countries as well. Though the population of the town is only around 36,000 (as per 2011 Census data), there are about 70,000 devotees visiting Shirdi every day. Due to this, the quantity of waste generated is very large. As a result, the town generates a huge quantity of garbage. However, the cleanliness of the town had been largely neglected. I resolved to prioritise this issue. Even though the Municipal Council collected this waste daily, the disposal of leftover food from restaurants has been a major challenge for the municipal authorities. This food waste is now transported to the biogas plant run by the Sansthan. A waste processing plant with the capacity of five tonnes has already been installed by the Sansthan. The Municipal Council is going to set up another such plant with equal processing capacity.

In response to Hon'ble Prime Minisater Narendra Modi's Swachh Bharat Abhiyan, with the initiative by the Municipal Council, 565 toilets were constructed for private use. The Sansthan spends crores of rupees on providing basic facilities, such as roads and electricity[29].

Tree Plantation

The unique feature of the Shirdi Municipal Council activities is the active participation of local citizens. Abhay and Yogita Shelke played a pivotal role in turning this into a movement. The clean-up movement is getting a good response from the citizens. A large number of school students participate in initiatives, such as tree plantation. The NGO

Green Shirdi Movement and the Shirdi Municipal Council in association with the Sansthan launched a tree plantation drive for a green Shirdi. Under this initiative, 10,000 trees have been planted in the Shirdi area and the Council has been successful in ensuring the survival of most of these trees.

Shirdi, the Cleanest Temple Town

In 2019, *India Today* carried out an extensive survey of all of the temple cities in India and found that Shirdi is the cleanest temple town. I received the first prize on behalf of the Sansthan at a grand function in the august presence of the Hon. President of India at New Delhi on 2nd October, 2019. I am satisfied to see that my vision of Clean Shirdi is becoming a reality.

Thus, we can see that waste management is vital in temple management. Shirdi has shown the way to other temple towns to become clean and green.

□

16

Power Management

Difficulties in life do not come to destroy you, but to help you realise your hidden potential and power. Let difficulties know that you too are difficult.

—Dr. A.P.J. Abdul Kalam[31]

Uninterrupted electric power supply is the necessity of any establishment. There were frequent power outages in Maharashtra some years back. There was a shortage of power generation. Load-shedding was a regular phenomenon, more common in villages and less visible in towns. But nowadays, the power supply position has improved and load-shedding has become history. Business output depends upon the availability of power; so does the functioning of temples.

Power Consumption

Let us take an example of the power situation in Sai Baba temple at Shirdi. The total estimated electrical power requirement is to the tune of 12 MWe and is drawn through transformers varying in capacities from 100 to 1000 KVA. The cost of power in Shirdi is around Rs. 10/- to 12/- per unit (1 kWHr). The annual cost of power consumption for the temple and for all the establishments, like *dharmashalas*, *prasadalaya*, hospitals, schools, water supply, etc. is around

Rs. 15 crores. The Sansthan has installed nine high voltage (11 kV) substations in various premises to draw power from the Maharashtra State Electricity Distribution Company Limited. The Sansthan also has installed 23 generators of varying capacities for power backup. Let me give you an idea of the power usage in Sai Sansthan.

Power Usage

Sai Sansthan manages accommodation facilities to house around 20,000 devotees (which includes Sai Nivas guesthouse, Shanti Nivas, Sevadham, Shantiniketan, Bhakta Niwas–500 rooms, Dwaravati, Sai Ashram, Sai Dharmashala); the mega kitchen having capacity to feed around one lakh devotees daily; two hospitals with a capacity of 575 beds; five educational institutions with a strength of around 6,000 students, staff quarters and other facilities. The Sansthan uses approximately 7,000 ceiling and other fans, 9,000 tubelights/LED lamps, 500 street lights, 950 air conditioners, 190 refrigerators, 300 TV sets, hundreds of lifts, around 265 computers, water pumps and other machinery.

Commercial Rates

Electricity supply to the temples is considered commercial and therefore it is charged at commercial rates. In my opinion, the power supplied to temples should not be considered commercial and it should be charged as per the rates applicable to residential premises.

Power Management[32]

Electric power management system (EPMS) of a building monitors the power- distribution system for usage and quality. The EPMS monitors the electrical distribution system, typically providing data on overall and specific power consumption, power quality and event alarms. Based on that data, the system can assist in defining and even initiating, schemes to reduce power consumption and power costs. The schemes 'shed' power and are triggered by predetermined thresholds, such as certain levels of power demand or a particular time of day when resource consumption is high. The EPMS can manage event alarms, calculate usage trends, track and schedule maintenance, troubleshoot, and 'bill back' metered power usage to specific users or tenants. The EPMS, together with the heating, ventilation and air conditioning (HVAC) system and the lighting control system are integral to overall energy management aimed at controlling usage and costs. In addition, the EPMS is a tool in managing and ensuring the quality of power, that is, a power source free from surges, sags and outages that may affect the facility's reliability and safety. Typical systems monitor the power service entrance of a building or campus, switchgear, generators, network protectors, switchboards, panel boards, uninterruptible power supplies (UPS) and emergency power generation.

Energy Management Systems[33]

As in the case of a PMS, an energy management system (EMS) can be used in two ways:

1. To assist the operator by monitoring and presenting data, including cost if necessary, by analysing this and advising actions to be taken to meet the criteria included in the predetermined data supplied to it.
2. To perform the above and, in addition, to implement automatic control of the system plant, such as generator sets and other energy sources, in accordance with its deduced analyses and conclusions. It will, of course, still function as a PMS to keep plants within designed operating limits, but such limits may have to differ from those used if it were performing solely as a PMS and not as an EMS.

Sources of Power at Sansthan

Wind Power[30]

In order to be self-sufficient in power and also to reduce the cost of power, the Sansthan has installed its own windmill of a capacity of 2MWe. The windmill is installed in the place where sufficient wind is available. The power thus produced is supplied to the power grid of Maharashtra government and the power is drawn from the grid at Shirdi. Government takes the charges for transmission of such power from its source to the destination at the pre-decided rate. This is called 'net-metering'. This helps is reducing the cost of power consumption by the Sansthan to the tune of Rs. 2 crores.

Solar Power[30]

The Sansthan has a plan for installation of a 10MWe solar power plant at a suitable location in Maharashtra. Nandurbar and Solapur are districts in Maharashtra that are preferred locations from the point of view of having suitable solar radiations. The estimated cost of the plant is around Rs. 40 crores. Detailed cost estimates have been approved by Maharashtra government. The tenders have been floated for supply and installation of such a plant, including purchase of the required land. Very soon it will become a reality. This will help in reducing the cost of power consumption by the Sansthan to the tune of Rs. 10 crores. Thus, with the help of windmill and solar plant, the Sansthan will becomes self-reliant vis-a-vis power. It has to bear only the transmission expenses of power from its source to Shirdi.

Rooftop Solar Plant

It was proposed to install a rooftop solar plant on the buildings owned by the Sansthan as it is comparatively cheaper and does not involve the cost of transmission. Initial study and estimation indicated that the said installation would not produce substantial power compared to the consumption by Sansthan. Secondly, some of the buildings of the Sansthan are heritage structures where such installation would not be permitted. Therefore, this idea was given up.

Every temple should see that it is self-sufficient in power supply. Even small temples can make use of the rooftop solar installation to fulfil their needs.

□

17

Infrastructure Management

Management works in the system;
leadership works on the system.

—Stephen Covey[3]

Infrastructure Management[34] (IM)

Infrastructure refers to the set of structures that are required for the operation of a physical facility or business operation. On a national or municipal level, the term 'infrastructure' refers to things like roads, sewers and drainage systems, water treatment facilities, bridges, tunnels, public transportation systems, airports, storage facilities and other components. In a physical facility like an office building, physical infrastructure consists of lighting, electricity, plumbing, alarm systems, electronic access and other features. The commonality here is that both physical and virtual infrastructure components are used by the people who manage them to deliver services that are crucial to the overall function and operations that characterise each location.

Problem Solving

Infrastructure solves problems; for example, plumbing infrastructure solves the problem of needing to get rid of human waste and electrical systems solve the need for power machines, electronics or appliances. A bridge solves the problem of needing to cross a river. The purpose of infrastructure management is to maintain infrastructure elements in acceptable working conditions so that they can be leveraged to solve the problem for which they were designed and implemented.

In the context of an IT organisation, infrastructure refers to the hardware, software and other systems that are necessary for delivering IT services in accordance with service-level agreements. IT Infrastructure management includes the management of IT policies and processes, along with the equipment, data, human resources and external contacts (such as vendors or security organisations) needed to ensure that IT operations run smoothly and efficiently.

IT Infrastructure management is sometimes divided into three components: systems management, storage management and network management. There are several defined categories of IT infrastructure elements that must be managed to ensure that critical applications remain available. The availability of cloud services has changed the way organisations manage their IT infrastructure, with an increasing number of infrastructure management tasks being outsourced to third-party managed service providers (MSPs). IT organisations can also invest in cloud-based infrastructure management tools to help simplify and streamline their infrastructure-management activities

At Shirdi

Sai Sansthan Shirdi has a good amount of both physical and IT infrastructure which caters to the needs of the devotees.

Roads

The Sansthan has built a number of roads in Shirdi, totalling a length of around 5,000 metres. Some of them are owned by the Sansthan, whereas, others are public roads owned by the Nagar Panchayat. There is no road-tax charged either by the Sansthan or by the Nagar Panchayat. The roads are maintained by the owners and the Sansthan also helps the

Nagar Panchayat in doing the job. The annual turnover of the Nagar Panchayat is not very large, about Rs. 40 to 50 crores. Moreover, the Sai Sansthan is morally and legally bound to support the activities of the Nagar Panchayat as it is stated in the Act specially prepared for working of the Sansthan.

Transport

Sai Sansthan has its own facilities for transport by buses and cars. The 23 number of public transport buses owned by the Sansthan are used for transporting devotees from the railway station or the bus stand to the *dharmashala*. In addition, the Sansthan uses 12 buses for transportation of school students. A number of 15 cars owned by the Sansthan are used by the officers and also for the guests. The Sansthan has an arrangement with the petrol pumps to supply petrol/ diesel on an annual basis through the tender system. The Sansthan's hospitals have 11 regular ambulances, one cardiac ambulance and one hearse.

Fire Brigade

The Sansthan has four fire-fighting vehicles. (1) *Water bowser*: It is a fully-automatic and state-of-the-art vehicle and has the capacity to hold 10,000 litres of water and 500 litres of foam. (2) *Foam tender*: It has the capacity to hold 4,500 litres of water and 500 litres of foam. (3) *Mini tender*: It has a capacity to hold 300 litres of water and 40 litres of foam. (4) *Fire bike*: It has the capacity to hold 40 litres of foam. In addition, the Nagar Panchayat has another fire tender with a capacity of 10,000 litres of water and 500 litres of foam to cater to the needs of the Sansthan and the town. They are manned by well-trained manpower and are ready to serve 24x7.

Lodging Facilities

The Sansthan has good facilities to house the devotees, right from dormitories to air-conditioned rooms. This has been explained in detail in a separate chapter in this book.

AIR FM Station

All India Radio station with FM 103.7 MHz frequency has become functional in Shirdi. There was a demand for it since the last 15 years but it materialised during the celebrations of Sai Baba's Samadhi Centenary in 2017-18. It does not have, at present, the capability of content generation. However, it broadcasts the programmes of AIR Nagar and also the *aartis* of the Sai temple on a daily basis. The Sansthan has provided the building and other facilities to the FM station. It is hoped that it will have its own team for content creation in the near future. This station has a range of 50 kms of periphery.

Free Wi-Fi

Shirdi has now become a Wi-Fi town with the provision of Wi-Fi facility to all the devotees and residents. Up to 15 MB data is provided per head per day, free of cost and it is charged thereafter.

Audio Video Telecasting

Sai Sansthan has video facilities for live transmission of the temple programmes on the television channel. Regular telecasts are made via the CCTV system of the Sansthan and the four large-sized LED screens installed in and around the temple premises.

Video Photography

Sai Sansthan has a special unit for videography and photography of the events and to cover celebrity visits. A well-trained staff with updated equipment operates the facilities for the benefit of the devotees.

Security and Surveillance

Sai Sansthan has a 24x7 security surveillance system through 310 CCTV cameras installed everywhere in the temple premises and also the physical security operated by about 962 trained security personnel. They help devotees to have a pleasant *darshan* experience.

Sai Museum

Sai Sansthan has a beautifully maintained museum that has preserved and displayed the clothes and other items used by Sai Baba. His original *kafni* (shirt) and *charan padukas* (shoes) are also displayed in this museum. It has original photographs of Sai Baba and his contemporaries.

Meditation Centre

Sai Sansthan has a well-crafted, soundproof meditation centre in the temple premises. It can accommodate around 200 devotees at a time and is open throughout the day. One can meditate here for as long as one wants. The centre has a very good ambience.

Proposed Facilities

Sai Sansthan has proposed a number of facilities to cater to the needs of the devotees, for instance, a Sai Knowledge Park containing a planetarium, Wax Museum, Star-gazing Gallery, a Holographic Show and so on. These are likely to see the light of the day in the near future.

□

18

Legal Management

Do not wait: the time will never be 'just right'. Start where you stand, and work whatever tools you may have at your command and better tools will be found as you go along.

—Napoleon Hill[35]

It is important to manage the ongoing legal cases of the organisation in all the courts. Now that most of the courts have become digital, tracking of cases online has become possible. Let us understand what legal management means.

Role of Legal Management[36]?

An advanced legal-case management software provides powerful administration and tracking of litigation processes and debt collection. With this solution, one can centralise legal processes data and documents, besides monitoring and controlling the cases. All the legal processes details and documents can be accessed securely, anywhere, besides managing the entire activity workflow processes in one system (all the information is secure at a centralised repository).

A legal management solution is specially designed to help law firms and other businesses.

The Legal Management System

This system makes complicated business processes

easier to manage by increasing the productivity and efficiency of the following departments:

- Legal affairs
- Operations
- Procurement
- Premises and security
- Compliance and IT

By centralising and integrating all the information, the legal management system enables better communication between different company departments and legal firms or legal firms and their clients, tracking important deadlines, managing cases, documents, expenses and collections.

At Shirdi

Ideally, there should be no court case against or by the organisation. A legal case does not arise overnight; it goes through a process. First, there arises a dispute between the parties. Discussions and deliberations take place between the parties. This important stage should not be missed by a clever legal manager. It is always cheaper to settle at this stage, though it may not be practically possible all the time. If there is no settlement on the issue, then a legal notice is sent by either party. This provides another opportunity to settle the dispute. If this is not availed of, then it culminates into a court case. Sai Sansthan has a load of as many as 67 court cases in various courts.

Court Cases

The court also offers the opportunity to settle the dispute and enter into a court consent. This court consent can be registered and it becomes a valid legal document. If there is no settlement at the early stage, the case continues and can go from District Court to High Court and then to the Supreme Court. It may take dozens of years. Experienced managers will agree with me that every case has to be settled at some or the other stage. Getting a decree from the court and executing it may take an indefinite period. But the initial enthusiasm of the parties has to come to an end or there has to be some mediation by influential persons known to both the parties. Thus, there is a time required for parties to come to a settlement. By this time, both the parties would have been drained by their respective advocates. It is to be noted that, in normal circumstances, no advocate will allow you to come to a settlement because he will lose his job. This is only to tell you that settle, settle and settle is the only way to resolve the court cases.

Legal Panel

The Sansthan has a legal panel of 33 advocates of the District and High Court to help resolve the legal disputes. There are many who aspire to be on the panel of the Sansthan, voluntarily or free of charge, just to enhance their profile.

Contract Agreements

Every work of the Sansthan is done through an execution of the contract. It is a legal document which governs the conditions of the contract. It is necessary that this document should be carefully prepared by specifying all the terms and conditions, so that there is no scope for dispute. Nothing should be left vague. Penalties and incentives should be specified in this contract. It is advisable to find out the legal history of the party before entering into the contract. By nature, some parties are found to be litigant, which should be avoided.

Purchase Orders

This is yet another legal document. The purchase order should clearly specify the quality or standard of the product, verification criteria, stages of payment, security deposit if any, place of delivery and so on. If the purchase order document is perfect, there is hardly any scope for the dispute or a court case.

However, in spite of taking all the care, one cannot guarantee that there will be no court case. One has to be prepared to face them and therefore, legal management becomes important.

Thus, legal management is an important aspect of temple management.

□

19

Technology in Management

Hard work never brings fatigue, it brings satisfaction.

—Narendra Modi[37]

Technology changes rapidly. It is necessary to keep pace with technology, else one will find that one is using almost outdated technology. We have to keep our eyes on the world and keep upgrading ourselves with the latest developments in technology.

What is Technology Management[38]?

Management of technology (MoT) can be viewed from different perspectives since the word technology itself is subject to various interpretations. The two terms, 'management' and 'technology', not only carry the burden of different meanings, but also present additional sophistication due their anthropological diversity. To many, MoT means managing engineering and technology; to others, MoT indicates managing knowledge and information, managing research and development, managing manufacture and operation, managing the activities of engineers and scientists or managing the functional activities without concern for the total activities that encompass the business concepts for the commercialisation process. According to Gaynor (1996), these interrelated activities must be integrated into a technology system. MoT means not only managing the system, but also managing the pieces involving integration of the 'pieces' into an acceptable 'whole' by focusing attention on the interdependence of the pieces. However, these elaborations are only part of the process of MoT. The important contributions to industry that management of technology can make are as follows:

- How to integrate technology into the overall strategic objectives of organisation.
- How to get into and out of technologies faster and more efficiently.
- How to assess/evaluate technology more efficiently.
- How best to accomplish technology transfer.
- How to reduce new product development's time and costs.
- How to manage large, complex and interdisciplinary or inter-organisational projects/systems.
- How to manage the organisation's internal use of technology.
- How to leverage the effectiveness of technical professionals.

To put it in a simple way, technology management is about getting people and technologies working together to do what people expect, which is a collection of systematic methods for managing the process of applying knowledge to extend the human activities and produce defined products. Effective technology management synthesises the best ideas from all sides: academic, practitioner, generalist or technologist.

At Shirdi

Technology plays an important role in management. At Shirdi, I have introduced maximum use of technology to provide succor to the devotees. Computerised biometric time slot *darshan* system, reverse osmosis-based water purification plant, air-conditioning of the *darshan* queue halls, digital photo/videography, transmission of live *darshan* signal to the TV channels, online reservation of accommodation, online donations, live *darshan* facility on mobile through Sai app, regular updating of the Sansthan website, making Shirdi a town with free Wi-Fi, AIR FM 103.7 station, proposed planetarium, holographic shows, anaerobic bio-digestion-based waste treatment plant and so on are some of the examples of usage of technology in the management of temple services.

□

Section-4

Darshan Management

20

Darshan Management

People will forget what you said,
People will forget what you did
But people will never forget how you made them feel.

—Maya Angelou[39]

Darshan is the most important part of the pilgrimage. Calm, peaceful and easy *darshan* is a satisfying experience.

Direct *Darshan*[30]

One scene in particular affected me deeply. In the midst of a queue, a lady was perched on a bench, hiding her face while she breastfed her infant. She was embarrassed by the crowd of men around her. She could not let her infant go hungry either, nor could she give up her place in the queue for *darshan*. The anguish of this mother disquieted me and I resolved that things needed an urgent change. There was a dire need for some basic and long-term facilities. I immediately decided that mothers with infants would be exempted from the queue and be allowed to get direct *darshan*. I also set up breastfeeding rooms for the mothers. A similar facility for direct *darshan* was provided for senior citizens, for devotees with medical conditions and handicaps. They too were exempted from the queue.

My Approach

Upon my appointment, I came to Shirdi and took charge as the chairman of the Sansthan. When I entered the town, I once witnessed the same lack of discipline and uncontrolled crowding as elsewhere. I went to the temple and directly joined the queue for *darshan*. People were crowding, pushing and shoving and using influence to get ahead in the queue. Employees, who recognised me, stared at me in surprise. Never before had they seen a chairman, who waited in the queue for *darshan*! While I progressed in the queue, I carefully observed the conditions around me. The discomfort faced by the devotees who had travelled hundreds of miles to get Sai *darshan* pained me. I could see crowding, unbearable heat, shortage of drinking water and inconvenience to babies, children and the aged. Agents were openly defying rules by trading VIP *darshan* passes and fleecing genuine devotees. All these things distressed me.

I keenly felt the need to address the poor conditions in the queue for *darshan*. Being a scientist, I pondered how technology could be used to address these problems.

When I reflected on what my primary duty as the chairman of the Sai Baba Sansthan was, I realised that it was to ensure a hassle-free and pleasant Sai Darshan experience for devotees. Board and lodging were supplementary facilities–the primary focus had to be on providing a pleasant *darshan* experience.

Darshan Experience

That first day, I somehow managed to get *darshan* and reached my office. The very first decision I took in the capacity of chairman was regarding the queue for *darshan*. Not just a *darshan*, I wanted to provide a pleasant *darshan* experience to the devotees. To ensure proper ventilation, I doubled the number of fans in the queue area, while replacing the old-fashioned windows with big glass-paned ones to ensure adequate light for the devotees. Air conditioning in the queue halls was provided.

A free-of-cost supply of tea, coffee, milk and biscuits to the devotees waiting in the queue and curbs on the sale of bottled water were put into place. An R.O. water purification plant was installed, and pure drinking water was made available to all the devotees, free of cost. The toilets in this area were absolutely filthy. We arranged for the cleaning of these toilets at regular intervals and retiled them to impart cleanliness and a better appearance.

Since a large number of devotees visit Shirdi daily, they had to wait in the queue for many hours to get *darshan*. To utilise this waiting time effectively, more than 300 LED closed-circuit TV monitors were installed along the *darshan* queue. They would run a live telecast of the Sai idol, *pooja, aarti, keertan* and *pravachan*. The devotees would get absorbed in the spiritual content being telecast and their waiting period turned pleasurable.

Darshan for Visually-impaired (blind) Persons

I would like to share with you my personal experience. Once, a large group of visually-impaired people visited the *mandir* for *darshan*. They expressed their joy and satisfaction at being allowed to take *darshan* directly on having been exempted from the queue. Somebody asked them, "You are unable to see Baba, then what did you gain by coming all the way here for *darshan*?" The reply given by one of them truly opened my eyes. He said, "It is true that we cannot see Baba, but isn't it sufficient that Baba can see us? It is enough for us that his gracious vision falls on us."

Computerised Time-slot *Darshan* Facility

Basic improvements, such as making the queue for *darshan* congenial and reducing the waiting time spent by devotees, were the need of the hour. With this in mind, I studied the *darshan* queue systems at various popular places of worship in India. I harnessed the latest technology and employed a computerised biometric time-slot system for *darshan*. To implement this system, around 40 computers were set up at various points around the *mandir* area. The devotees are registered first, computerised photograph is clicked and fingerprint impressions are recorded. Then they are issued a pass for *darshan* within a time slot. Devotees can obtain this pass as soon as they arrive in Shirdi. They are then allotted a fixed time slot for *darshan*, so that they can manage the rest of their schedule and arrive in the *darshan* queue at the given time. While joining the queue, every pass is scanned. It is also scanned at the exit after *darshan*, so that a record of the time required to obtain *darshan* for each devotee is created. It was found that on an average, it took around 45 minutes for the devotee to get the *darshan*. And they need not stand in queues for six or seven hours any more. The system works on the estimation that an average of 6,000 devotees get *darshan* every hour. Another advantage of this system was that we could record the exact number of visiting devotees. Earlier, these numbers were only rough estimates.

This was a revolutionary change that we introduced. Now, an online booking facility has also been made available for the visiting devotees.

The Sai Baba Sansthan Mandir was awarded the ISO certification by the government for excellent management. As a result, the facilities for *pooja* and other rituals have been authenticated and standardised. Now a devotee can book his *darshan* and accommodation as also his train tickets.

Making VIP *Darshan* Open to All

I took charge with the determination to bring in transparent functioning in all systems. One negative aspect about Shirdi had caught my attention as soon as I arrived. In a way, unsuspecting devotees were being looted. There was a facility to obtain a VIP pass for immediate *darshan* by donating Rs. 200/- to the *mandir*. However, for this VIP pass, one also required a letter of recommendation from an MLA, MLC, MP, a minister or a local leader. A whole gang of agents supplying such letters of recommendation would move around the *mandir* trying to rope in innocent and unsuspecting devotees and fleece them of hundreds of rupees in exchange for these letters. They would charge Rs. 1,000/- for the pass that cost only Rs. 200/-. They were running a wide and well-entrenched racket. The Public Relations Office, where such passes were issued, would always be crowded with agents. I immediately resolved to do away with the requirement of any recommendation letter for obtaining a VIP *darshan* pass. A number of people, including some officials, warned me, "Do not take such a decision. It will have negative effects; you will face tremendous opposition." In a way, they attempted to pressurise me into changing my mind, but I did not pay heed to them. I believed that the fleecing of devotees must be stopped and I took a firm stand. I took the trustees into confidence and stopped this obnoxious practice. I removed the necessity of recommendation letters for getting a VIP *darshan* pass, thus making the facility available to all.

I ordered that the paid VIP passes be made available on demand to anyone. Online booking of such passes was also started. This proved to be a boon for devotees who are pressed for time. The agents crowding around the Public Relations Office disappeared. I was waiting for a backlash, but no one opposed me. Many people were worried that such a step might affect the revenue flowing into the Sansthan. In actual fact, the *mandir* was earning around Rs. 18 crores (Rs. 180 million) annually through the sale of VIP passes. In the first year after my decision, the revenue jumped to Rs. 43 crores (Rs. 430 million), and in the year after that, it reached Rs. 61 crores (Rs. 610 million). Thus, the huge amount of money which was being diverted from *mandir* revenues was secured. I was successful in curbing the loot of devotees and the rampant corruption being carried out in the name of VIP *darshan*.

When the VIP pass facility was offered to the public, in the first year, 21.5 lakh (2.15 million) devotees benefited from it. In the next year, 30.5 lakh (3.05 million) devotees opted for these passes. Under this facility, devotees can obtain *darshan* within 15 to 20 minutes. Now, while booking railway tickets to Shirdi from anywhere in the country, devotees can also book a *darshan* time-slot. This facility is being offered in cooperation with the railways. Thousands of devotees avail this facility.

Modern *Darshan* Queue Complex Project

In consultation with the trustees, we prepared a plan to improve the *darshan* facilities. This plan was named the Modern *Darshan* Queue Complex. In order to make the Sai Darshan process pleasant and comfortable for devotees, the Sansthan is building a well-equipped fully air-conditioned Darshan Queue Complex at the location of the old *prasadalaya*. The main building of the Darshan Queue Complex will occupy an area of 20,082 sq. mtrs. The ground floor will have an area of 6,581 sq. mtrs., while both the first and second floors will have an area of 6,133 sq. mtrs. each. This building will contain three large entrance halls that will be well-equipped with facilities, such as mobile phone and footwear storage lockers, 48 biometric pass-issuing counters, 20 paid pass-issuing counters, 10 counters for sale of *ladoos*, 10 counters for *udi* (sacred ash) and *kapad-kothi*, 10 bookstalls, a donation office, a tea and coffee counter, separate washrooms for men and women, spacious lifts, R.O.-purified drinking water, proper ventilation, fire-fighting equipment, security check, etc. This building will contain a total of 12 halls, which will be able to accommodate a total of 18,000 devotees. This project would cost Rs. 10 crores (Rs 1.10 billion) and the work is at an advanced stage. This complex is connected directly to the *mandir* through a skywalk.

Mukh Darshan Facility

Every devotee longs for *darshan*, but not all have enough time. These are the devotees who fall prey to corrupt practices. Having observed this, I contemplated a solution to the problem. The idea of introducing *mukh darshan* suddenly came to mind. Devotees who were pressed for time could avail the joy of *mukh darshan* at least. So, I made arrangements for the same at the front of the *mandir*.

Booking *Darshan* with Railway Ticket

I had presented a request to the then Minister for Railways Piyush Goyal to allow devotees travelling to Shirdi by train to book *darshan* passes at the time of booking their travel tickets. He immediately granted the request. Due to his speedy implementation, this facility was offered to devotees starting from 26th January 2019. Around 57 trains arrive at or pass through Shirdi station every week. Now all the devotees travelling by these trains can book *darshan* passes along with their railway tickets.

□

21

Management of Donations

Let us sacrifice our today so that our children can have a better tomorrow.

—A.P.J. Abdul Kalam[40]

Donations constitute the major source of income for any temple. Therefore, one finds that almost all the temples have donation boxes kept along the passage in the temple premises. Nowadays, because of the digital revolution many other options for cash donations are available, like RTGS, NEFT, PhonePe, online payment gateways, credit/debit cards. Furthermore, there could be different appeals to the devotees to donate for various causes, which may have selective effects. Let us understand the existing sources and the possible modes of increasing the income of the temples.

Donation Boxes

Shri Sai Baba Sansthan Shirdi has 52 donation boxes in the temple premises to help devotees to donate as per their wish. Sai temple has an international appeal. Non-resident Indians as well as foreign nationals visit Shirdi for Baba's *darshan*. People donate money in rupees as well as in currencies of different countries. It is estimated that Sai temple gets donations in the currencies of 43 countries. All the donations get converted and are deposited in the banks. Some devotees donate by way of gold, silver, brass, copper in these donation boxes. Letters to Sai Baba are also found in the boxes, at times. There is a well-developed system of counting the donations in the temple and this has been separately explained.

Online Donations

Online payment gateways are made available by the temple through various nationalised and private banks. NEFT/RTGS facilities are also available for donations. People can login to the website of the Sansthan, wherein to make online donations. There are donation counters in the temple premises at Shirdi where people walk in and pay either by cash or by credit/debit cards. On my first visit to Sai Baba temple after taking charge, I asked about the donation counters. They were located in some corners of the premises. I brought them to the front so that they would be easily visible to the devotees. I also got the counters refurbished to improve the ambience. I also asked the persons in charge of the donation counters to arrange some flower bouquets/garlands from the *Samadhi Mandir* and honour the devotees who made donations at the counters. They also take photographs to provide to the donors.

Return Gift

I thought of giving return gifts to the donors. We decided to give silver *padukas* embossed on silver coins weighing 20 g to the devotees paying more than Rs. 25,000/- by way of donation. It proved a pleasant emotional surprise for the devotees who felt as if they were carrying Baba with them to their homes. They would worship those *padukas* every day at home.

Donation Counting Hall

This is yet another unique facility in the temple premises. The donations received by the temple in cash or kind are deposited in the *hundis* or donation boxes. There are 47 such donation boxes in the temple. The donation counting methodology is highly transparent. Devotees, villagers, employees and banks participate in this process. There is a large hall in the basement of the temple. All the donation boxes are opened on the ground floor in the presence of witnesses and they are emptied into a tunnel. Through that, the donations go to the counting hall in the basement. There are appointed representatives and bank employees in this hall for segregating the items into notes, coins, metal, coins of different countries. The coins are normally counted by weighing machines and packed. Such weighted packets are handed over to the bank as they are. All the people in this hall wear a special uniform of half-sleeved shirt and *pyjama*. The uniform is designed in such a manner that it has no pockets, no collar and no place to hide anything. They are checked by security personnel on entry and exit and they cannot leave the hall until the entire process is completed. After counting, the money is handed over to the bank present on that day. They issue receipts, collect the money and leave for their destination. As many as 15 banks are involved in this process and they are given the work by turns. The counting takes place twice a week, on Tuesdays and Fridays. The amount so received is around Rs. 2 to 3 crores in every counting and is displayed at the donation counter. This place is not open to visitors.

Transparency

The process of counting is carried out under closed circuit television (CCTV) cameras and is also recorded. The process is fully transparent and foolproof beyond doubt. The donation amount, so collected and displayed on the boards, leaves no scope for suspicion. This practice is worth being adopted by all the temples.

Donation Schemes

Different people respond to different appeals. Therefore, temple authorities should think of everyone while designing the donation schemes. The following schemes may be thought of with modifications to suit a particular temple:

1. ***Annadaan* Scheme:** A large section of people respond to appeals for *annadaan* (donation of food). It is about feeding the hungry. Many temples have adopted this *annadaan* scheme. One can appeal to the people to donate a day's *annadaan* on the occasion of their birthday or anniversary, by specifying the budget. The names of such donors could be displayed on boards, CCTVs or announced to give him/her credit for that day's *annadaan*. At Shirdi, the food is being served free of cost from 1st January 2017 at the *prasadalaya*; earlier, it was charged. The scheme as stated above was introduced among the devotees. They were requested to donate and book the day they wanted to offer *annadaan*. It was surprising to find that within a short period of time, 250 out of 365 days were booked by the devotees, with a day's expense of Rs.5.50 lakhs. This scheme became very popular. In addition, one can donate any small or large amount to the *annadaan* scheme and it is deposited under that head and used for the said purpose.
2. **Healthcare:** Sai Baba Sansthan is running two large-sized state-of-the-art hospitals with a total capacity of 575 beds. The devotees can donate funds towards healthcare and these funds are utilised for the said purpose. Many temples already have small or medium-sized healthcare facilities or even an OPD to serve the poor patients, and if not, they can introduce this service. Donors cannot locate the poor and needy persons. Therefore, the temple can become the provider of such facilities to the devotees whereby they could donate and earn satisfaction. See the interesting phenomenon. The devotee donates money, the temple gives him/her blessings and she/he gets satisfaction. There is an exchange of intangible things for tangible ones. People donate for such schemes. Depending on the requirement, somebody can donate

a building, someone else can donate machinery and others can even give their name to the facility. It is a human instinct to be remembered after death by way of offering good services to society.

3. **Education:** Health and education are the two sectors which are often beyond the budget of the common man. Therefore, these two are the reasons where the maximum number of people look for help and relief. The temple can run educational institutions and provide quality education at an affordable price. The Sai Baba Sansthan is running five educational institutions, described separately in this book, for the benefit of the poor and needy. All temples can take up some activity in the field of education, depending on the local needs and receive blessings from the society.
4. **Others:** Similarly, one can organise literary classes, or on eradication of poverty, removal of superstitions, organ donation scheme, blood donation scheme, library, mobile laboratory in rural areas, job-oriented courses, business-oriented courses and mentoring.

The list could be endless, so long as one has a vision to look for a gap and try to fill up that gap. In a nutshell, one can help in elevating the life and living of the downtrodden or of a person standing at the bottom of the pyramid.

□

22

Prasad Management

The world's hunger is getting ridiculous. There is more fruit in the rich man's shampoo than in a poor man's plate.

—Unknown[41]

Prasadalaya Serves Food as Blessings of Sai Baba[30]

Management of food *prasad* for 70,000 to 100,000 people every day is a massive challenge. At Shirdi *prasadalaya*, which has been serving devotees for a number of years now, this task is accomplished with ease. The grace of Sai is evident from the fact that not a single devotee leaves the *prasadalaya* without a meal. The *prasad* is now being offered entirely free of cost from 1st January 2017. A mega kitchen runs on solar energy. National Geographic channel took notice of it and rightly telecasted the story which was appreciated throughout the world. A brief overview of the project is given here.

When I visited the *prasadalaya*, I was astounded at the sheer scale of work that is required daily. The *prasadalaya* is the kitchen where meals for 70,000 to one lakh devotees are cooked and served daily. On festive days, the number of meals cooked rises to more than one lakh. Since food is prepared on a huge scale, there are possibilities of error and food wastage. Cooking and serving food is a laborious task. I was struck by the thought that the latest machines could be harnessed to lighten some of the workload. I decided to bring in machines to make *chapatis*, chop vegetables and wash the plates and bowls. The newly procured *chapati*-making machine makes 25,000 *chapatis* every hour. When the vision is progressive, its impact is assuredly positive.

Food Wastage

On observing that a huge amount of food was being wasted daily at the *prasadalaya*, a proper survey was conducted. I learned that the daily food wastage amounted to around five tonnes. After a detailed study, I came up with certain solutions to address the issue. I found that the servers in the *prasadalaya* were serving large helpings to each devotee to minimise the number of times they had to walk among the tables. This led the devotees to waste food because they could not finish all the food that was served. Trolleys were being used to carry the food to the tables, but the wheels of the trolleys malfunctioned. So, the servers were stationing the trolley at one point and carrying the food from there to the tables, which resulted in a lot of spillage. The floor tiles in the *prasadalaya* had cracked, thereby obstructing and damaging the trolley wheels.

Reducing Wastage

I had the wheels of all the trolleys replaced with ball bearings and got the floor tiles replaced with sturdy 65-mm granite flooring. Now, the trolleys can be wheeled around smoothly. I replaced the big serving spoons and ladles with smaller ones. The size of the bowls meant for serving *dal* and vegetables was also reduced.

Wastage was also caused because the food items were excessively spicy. It was decided that the food would be made less spicy and that green chillies would be served to those who requested for spicier food. Sai *sevaks* (volunteers) with plaques stating 'This food is *prasad*. Please do not waste it' were deputed to walk among the tables. They started requesting devotees to not leave food on their plates. As a cumulative effect of these measures, the food wastage was reduced from

5 tonnes to just 0.75 tonnes per day–a whopping 85 per cent reduction in wastage. This meant that the food wastage per head reduced to only 19g. Employees are striving towards zero food wastage. The person in charge of the *prasadalaya*, Shri Vishnu Thorat, is a wonderful person who takes a keen interest in reducing food wastage. A significant quantity of food is being saved from wastage every day.

Annadaan Scheme

Trustees of the Sai Baba Sansthan have also introduced a food donation (*annadaan*) scheme for devotees, who are appealed to donate food any one day per year, or on their birthday or the anniversary of a loved one. The daily cost of serving food at the *prasadalaya* comes to Rs. 5.5 lakh rupees. When a devotee donates this amount, the food served on that particular day is served in their name. Their name is displayed on TV screens in the premises of the *mandir* and of the *prasadalaya*. This scheme has garnered tremendous response. Devotees have donated an amount for food service for as many as 250 days in a year.

Round-the-clock Kitchen

The growing number of visiting devotees is a challenge and the Sansthan has brought in ultra-modern equipment to meet it. A system for cooking by using solar energy had already been installed. Retrofittings on this system have been implemented. Thus, devotion is reinforced by technology and the devotees, for whom the act of eating *prasad* is also a form of worship, are satisfied. Daily, the work in the kitchen begins at 2 a.m. and continues right up to 11 p.m. It stops for only three hours every night, and that too for the daily cleaning.

A visit to the *prasadalaya* in Shirdi proves that even immense tasks become simple through the grace of Sai. Serving food to the hungry was a special aspect of Sai Baba's service. Even today, no one, who visits the *prasadalaya*, goes away hungry.

Mega Kitchen

From the beginning, the trustees had emphasised the use of latest technology for the efficient functioning of this mega kitchen. A large solar steam cooking plant has been installed in the *prasadalaya* and 2,000 kg of food grains are cooked here daily. This plant, which was installed at the cost of Rs. 1.33 crores (Rs. 13.3 million), has led to conservation of huge amounts of cooking gas. This project has received a grant from the Central Ministry of New and Renewable Energy. In addition to this, two containers with a capacity of 10 metric tonnes each have been installed to meet the daily requirement of cooking gas. An automatic *chapati*-making machine, manufactured by Prama Kitchen Equipment, has been installed to make *chapatis*. Three dough-kneading machines are used, each of them capable of kneading 40 kg of dough in 10 minutes. Prior to kneading, there are machines at every step–for cleaning stones from wheat and for grinding wheat into flour. The entire system is such that one can pour wheat into the machines at one end and receive hot readymade *chapatis* brushed with *ghee* at the other end of the process.

Big machines have been installed to automate the processes of washing and chopping vegetables and cleaning the used plates and bowls. German dishwashers manufactured by Hobart have been installed. An ultra-modern fire-prevention security system has been installed in the kitchen. The quality and hygiene of food prepared is strictly controlled. Around 800 people are employed to work in the *prasadalaya*.

Shirdi is now known worldwide as devotees from every corner of the world pay a visit. *Sai Mandir* has a special place in the hearts of millions who throng every year. Shirdi is constantly setting new records vis-à-vis the number of visitors.

Comfortable *Darshan*

Ensuring easy, happy and smooth *darshan* for visiting devotees is the priority of the Sansthan. Equal emphasis is placed on ensuring that the visiting devotees receive proper facilities and complete the pilgrimage to Shirdi in comfort. Devotees come to Shirdi from all parts of India. Many of them hail from a poor background. It is important to provide them with good facilities for board and lodging. The Trustees have faced this challenge with a positive attitude and detailed planning. The infrastructure has been so laid that food and accommodation are provided to the rapidly growing numbers. The most outstanding service-provider is the *prasadalaya*. The food served here is seen as a blessing of Sai Baba himself. His grace is such that any shortage is never experienced here. Sai Baba himself always cared for the hungry and feeding them was his unique trait. He would not eat his own meals unless he had fed the hungry–not just hungry people, but also cats and dogs. Donating food was a special aspect of his service. Even today, at Shirdi, we practise his *mantra* of donating food. Every devotee who eats at the *prasadalaya* experiences divine satisfaction.

Free Food

In most of the large temples in India, visiting devotees are served free-of-cost meals. This system is efficiently implemented at Shegaon and Akkalkot in Maharashtra. Implementing provision of free food at Shirdi was an immense challenge due to the sheer number of devotees visiting daily. But the Trustees were determined to continue Baba's tradition of feeding the hungry and of serving the sick. So, we employed the latest technology and made continuous improvements for the benefit of the devotees. This facility is provided at the *mandir* and at various points near the residential accommodations. In addition to feeding devotees, the *prasadalaya* also serves midday meals to thousands in old-age homes and local schools for visually-challenged and *divyang* students as these are located in and around Shirdi.

The newly-constructed *prasadalaya*, which cost around Rs. 22 crores (Rs. 220 million), was dedicated to the public on 8th January 2009. Special dining halls have been constructed for devotees at the main *prasadalaya*, the Sai Baba *bhakta-niwas*, the Dwarawati *bhakta-niwas* and the Sai Ashram *bhakta-niwas*. The main *prasadalaya* as well as these dining halls serve meals from 10 a.m. to 10 p.m. A wholesome complete meal consisting of *chapatis* or *puris*, vegetables, rice, pulses, *dal* or *sambar* is served. This mega kitchen utilises around 30 quintals of rice and 40 quintals of wheat daily. Pulses, vegetables and other ingredients are used in proportionately large quantities.

ISO Kitchen

The *prasadalaya* has been awarded an ISO certification for maintaining quality and for efficient functioning. It is the first kitchen in Asia to receive this prestigious certificate. It also received a special award from the Ministry of New and Renewable Energy in 2013 for being the largest solar energy project run by a religious institution. In 2013, the state government also presented the Sansthan with an award for energy conservation and promotion of solar energy. However, the true certificate of the efficiency of the *prasadalaya* is the satisfaction on the faces of the devotees who eat here.

Udi Management

Udi produced in the sacred fire (*dhuni*) at Dwarkamai in *Samadhi Mandir* is considered as Baba's *prasad* and so is sacred with divine powers. Thus every devotee visiting Shirdi would like to get *udi prasad*. There was a shortage of *udi prasad* in the temple and I have explained in an earlier chapter how this was resolved. Now it is ensured that every devotee gets *udi prasad* right after the *darshan* and there is no separate queue for that. Happiness is expressed by devotees regarding this facility.

Prasad management is an integral part of temple management.

□

23

Lodging Management

People throw stones at you and you convert them into milestones.

—Sachin Tendulkar[42]

Temple tourism has been very popular in India since ancient times. Devotees go for *Char Dham yatra*, where the destinations are in four different directions of the country. People visit Kumbh Mela, which is held in 12 different parts of India in rotation and is held at the same place every 12 years; then the 12 *jyotirlinga* (*Shivalinga*) *yatra, Ashtavinayak yatra* and so on are also popular. Lodging is an inevitable requirement of this religious tourism.

Lodging Management[43]

Imagine visiting your favourite temple, for which you have been planning for a few months and you are looking forward to having a great time. Apart from the destination, *darshan* and the food are likely to be your major concern during the trip. After spending quality time at the temple and the town, you will obviously want to feel comfortable in the room or your cottage where you can rest. Accommodation is one of the components of travel that can make the experience more cheerful and memorable.

Tourism industry in India is growing at a rapid pace, contributing about 6-7 per cent of national GDP and the numbers are expected to improve in the years to come. Tourism and hospitality management courses, though in their nascent stages (as compared to engineering and commerce courses), have been drawing the attention of the young generation, thanks to the positive outlook of the sector. Today, there are many colleges, institutes and universities offering courses in tourism management.

Indian Hospitality Industry–Current Status

Hospitality is among the top sectors in India that has attracted investment in recent times. The Ministry of Tourism has taken many steps to promote tourism in the nation. Maharashtra, Tamil Nadu, Uttar Pradesh and Goa have taken initiatives to improve the infrastructure in their respective states to attract travellers. In the hospitality industry, the lodging business is a key area where many corporate houses have made large investments. While there are many home-grown renowned brands which are expected to expand their base in the nation, there are many international brands, such as Marriott and Keys Hotels, which are planning to start new hotels in different parts of India. Added to this, there are many investment companies that have invested money in the hotel industry and have been acquiring travel portals. All these factors create a positive outlook for the future of the hospitality sector in the nation.

Accommodation–How it Impacts Tourism?

Accommodation is one of the basic necessities of international and domestic travellers. A government which is focused on developing tourism in the state normally considers reducing tax and increasing incentives for hotels or businesses that provide accommodation in travel destinations. This can promote the construction of new hotels or resorts in the locality, driving the growth of the tourism sector. To ensure good travelling experience, it is important for hotels to have well-set quality standards for operations and safety, hygiene and health policies. An accommodation manager is trained to take care of the quality standards, manage budget and staff and plan business in hotels, resorts or any other tourism business he/she is working with. Students learn the vital quality guidelines, human resource management skills and other managerial aspects of the job profile during their graduation or post-graduation courses.

Accommodation Management–What does it Involve?

Accommodation plays a major role in a traveller's overall experience of visiting a place. It is one of the big components of traveller's expenditure. Therefore, the role of accommodation manager is crucial in the hotel business/ tourism industry. Accommodation manager mainly deals with human resources, budget and inventory. It is his/her responsibility to get the staff trained and ensure that quality standards for hygiene, health and safety are met in the hotel environment. Maintenance of the infrastructure too falls under the purview of the manager. Since the professional deals with staff and with customers, it is important for him/her to have a positive attitude, higher energy, good communication skills and relationship management skills, knowledge of handling finances and budget and integrity. The manager's services directly impact the hotel as a brand. When performed well, accommodation management can bring back customers to a hotel or resort for the second, third and multiple number of times. Customer satisfaction and wonderful memories are intangible takeaways for customers that can greatly impact the business's growth.

Lodging Facilities by the Sansthan at Shirdi

Sai Sansthan has a number of lodges or *dharmashalas* to accommodate devotees visiting Shirdi. Sai Ashram, I also know of *dharmashalas* with 1,000 rooms, but the *dharmashala* in Shirdi is biggest with 1,536 rooms. Each room can house two or three guests. It has a number of buildings with ground plus four storeys. Some of the rooms are air-conditioned. Sai Ashram-II or Sai *dharmashala* also has a number of ground plus four-storey buildings and all the rooms are not air conditioned. It has around 192 dormitories, each one having the capacity to accommodate around 20 guests. They have cots, beds and lockers with common toilets. Sai Ashram-II can house more than 3,840 guests. Then there are other buildings, viz. Dwaravati with 320 rooms, Sai Bhakta Nivas with 560 rooms, Sai Dham, Sai Nivas with 24 semi-luxury rooms, Sai Niketan and so on to accommodate the guests. The overall capacity of the Sansthan is to accommodate around 20,000 devotees in all the buildings. The tariff is highly reasonable as compared to private accommodation, varying from Rs. 10/- per day to Rs. 800/- per day. This tariff also regulates the tariff of private hotels in Shirdi.

Check-in Process

In one of my visits to these *dharmashalas*, I noticed that there were a number of guests waiting to get accommodated. They had arrived at the *dharmashala* at 5.00 a.m. and were kept waiting because the check-in time decided by the management was 10.00 a.m. Most of the trains arrive at Shirdi in the early morning hours. I immediately asked the managers to accommodate the guests as and when they arrive and not keep them waiting. The check-in timing was changed to 5.00 a.m. for all the guests.

The Sansthan accommodation can be booked online. However, considering that there are some devotees who are not well-versed with the online system, some accommodation (around 10 per cent) is kept on hold for the direct arrivals.

Private Lodging

Shirdi also has huge private accommodation facilities. There are around 3,000 small and big hotels in Shirdi. Their sizes vary from 20 rooms to 200 rooms and the tariff also depends on the facilities provided. The capacity of all the hotels together is to accommodate around 58,000 guests.

Thus, Shirdi Sai Sansthan and the hotels together can provide lodging to around 78,000 guests. This much is sufficient on usual days, but during festival days the number of devotees pouring into Shirdi rises to 2 lakhs, and then the system collapses. There is a lot of competition among the hoteliers. The agents who provide customers to the hotels get paid well, to the tune of 40 per cent of the tariff. They are called 'polishwale'. The moment you enter Shirdi, these 'polishwale'. will approach you for accommodation. They can pick you up from the railway station, or bus stand and take you to the hotel of their choice. The hotel tariff is not fixed, barring for a few exceptions; it varies, depending upon the demand-supply position.

Banquet Halls

There are around 400 private banquet halls in Shirdi, of different sizes. Most of them are attached to the hotels. This makes Shirdi a centre for destination weddings and business conferences. Corporates prefer to have their annual functions or training camps in Shirdi.

Canteens

All the *dharmashalas* have canteens attached. They serve food that is cooked in the mega kitchen at *prasadalaya*. This service is made available to the devotees.

Transport

Suitable transport arrangements are made for the devotees to commute between the *dharmashalas* and the temple, the hospitals, the railway station or bus stand. This transport is provided free of cost.

Thus, lodging management is an important part of temple tourism and temple management. People have *astha* (faith) in the deity but good accommodation, transport facilities and clean *prasadalaya* create and enhance the *astha* manifold about the pilgrim town.

□

Section-5

Social Management

24

Management of Education

If we want to reach real peace in this world,
we should start educating children.

—Mahatma Gandhi[44]

Education and healthcare are the two very important sectors to build the future of any nation. The expenses of these services are becoming beyond the reach of the poor. It is not that free education facilities are not available in the country, but the situation is pathetic. Till the emergence of private educational institutions based on capitation fees, the education field matured with dedicated teachers. When education was commercialised, the dedicated teachers went on backfoot. The educational facilities of the Sansthan at Shirdi are almost free of cost for students, yet the teachers are well-paid. A good amount of dedication is seen in the teachers and they impart quality education. This has become possible only by subsidising it through the resources of the temple. Therefore, management of education will play an important role in temple management.

Towards Modernity through Education[30]

Education is given a special focus among the various initiatives run by Shri Sai Baba Sansthan. Schools and colleges have been offering education for many years. The development of a new modern educational complex, spanning over 7.0 lakh sq. ft. of construction with a project cost of Rs. 218 crores (Rs. 2.18 billion), is nearing completion.

Through his own life, Sadguru Sai Baba created ideals of social service and education. Inspired by his ideals, the Sai Sansthan has fulfilled its social commitment by setting up model educational institutions. The schools and colleges managed by the Sansthan are making exemplary progress; particularly the ITI has set new standards all over India.

I firmly believe that education is the only way one can shape the future. I myself was able to overcome challenging circumstances on the strength of my education. I sincerely wanted to provide the latest educational facilities to students in the Shirdi area through the educational institutions. Shirdi was blessed by Sai Baba's residence, but it has remained underdeveloped in other aspects. I was confident that, given proper education, the children of Shirdi would transform the face of the town. Hence, after the *darshan* facilities and medical facilities, I focused my attention and efforts on the educational facilities.

Five Institutions

The Sansthan has always prioritised educational initiatives. The Sansthan, at present, runs five educational institutions in Shirdi–Shri Sai Baba Kanya Vidyamandir (a girls' school), Shri Sai Baba English Medium School (junior kindergarten to Standard X), Junior College, Industrial Training Institute (ITI) and Degree College.

Currently, more than 6,000 students are studying in these institutions. They are receiving high-quality education at very low costs. The poor and needy are benefiting greatly from this initiative. So far, the schools/colleges of the Sansthan were functioning in the premises of the *dharmashala*.

Degree College

The Degree College managed by the Sansthan has started

functioning and was the first significant necessary step in the direction of educational progress. It has helped poor students and especially the girls to continue their education till obtaining the degree. Shri Sai Baba Sansthan planted the seeds of education in a small town that did not have access to many facilities. The newly-opened Degree College has three faculties–arts, science and commerce. Even after sustained efforts by many over 15 years, the vision of this Degree College could not become a reality. The Board of Trustees, particularly vice president Chandrashekhar Kadam and other senior officials, took untiring efforts. With orders from the then Chief Minister Hon'ble Devendra Fadnavis and the then Education Minister Shri Vinod Tawde, the Degree College was opened in 2018. These educational institutions have created a unique identity by offering high-quality education.

UPSC/MPSC Training

I also proposed setting up a free-of-cost training centre in Shirdi for UPSC/MPSC competitive exams. The building is ready and the centre will benefit students from rural areas. Shri Sudheer Thakare, former chairman of MPSC has been appointed as chairman of the governing council of the centre. It is expected to become functional soon.

Modern Education Complex

I envisioned a well-equipped modern educational complex at Shirdi and I began to take planned steps towards achieving this goal. The Board of Trustees decided that, in order to provide students with a conducive atmosphere for quality education, a modern educational complex should be set up. I had the vision of a single educational complex housing the schools, colleges, ITI, library, laboratory, hostel, playground and auditorium. A budget of Rs. 218 crores (Rs. 2.18 billion) was set aside for this project and 18 acres of land earmarked for the complex. The project design was prepared. The work order for the same was issued after completing a transparent e-tender process. The construction is in an advanced stage and is expected to be completed within the next two to three months.

This complex has spacious buildings to house all the necessary institutions, including a separate school for girls, a well-stocked library, fully equipped laboratories, a playground for sports, a swimming pool, facilities for indoor games, a teachers' common room, an auditorium with a seating capacity of 1,200 and a separate hall for educational and cultural activities. This complex will aim at widening the horizons of knowledge and science. Students from the surrounding areas will benefit from these facilities. They will get significant opportunities to excel at education as well as in sports.

Bhoomi Poojan by Hon'ble Prime Minister

Hon'ble Prime Minister Shri Narendra Modi visited Shirdi on 19th October, 2018 to lay the foundation stone of the modern educational complex project spread over 18 acres of land and having a built-up area of around 7.0 lakh sq.ft. He took detailed information on the proposed plans for the same. This project is rapidly taking shape and by the time this book is published, the development of the modern educational complex would have reached completion.

Sai Baba came to a small town like Shirdi and as a result, Shirdi was transformed. Baba set ideals of social service, education and healthcare, thereby inspiring lakhs of devotees to follow in his footsteps. The combined efforts of skilled administrators and dedicated teachers helped in the growth of the sapling that the Sai Baba had planted.

'A' Grade Industrial Training Institute (ITI)

The ITI managed by Sai Baba Sansthan occupies a pride of place among all the educational institutions. Under the leadership of Principal Shivalinga Patne, students have established new records and have won renown at the national level. Shri Sai Baba ITI was established on 1st August, 1984. This government-recognised institute is regarded as top-ranking among private industrial training institutes. It has received the 'A' grade among private institutes.

From four initial trades, the ITI now offers training for 11 trades, such as electrician, mechanic motor vehicle, mechanic tractor, fitter, welder, turner, mechanic RAC, tool and die maker, computer operator, programming assistant and machinist grinder as well as training in the fields of information technology and communication system maintenance. There are 22 divisions for these trades and training is given in two shifts. Two workshops are set up for the trainees to perform practicals. The institute has seats for 450 trainees. All admissions are conducted online and on merit basis as per the norms of the state government. Due to the online system, there is no scope for favouritism or nepotism in the admission process. I am proud to state that the educational institutions in Shirdi are free from corruption.

90 Per Cent Placement

Compared to other educational institutions, the fees charged by Sansthan are very low. The state government norms allow a 20 per cent management quota, but these management seats are also transferred to the government and all admissions are made as per common rules. As much as 90 per cent of the successful students get a placement. This is probably the only ITI where graduates get a placement.

In 2013-2014, the government increased the tuition fees, but the Sai Baba ITI retained its old fee structure. As a result, the Sansthan gives a total fee waiver of around Rs. 92 lakhs (Rs. 9.2 million) to trainees every year.

Since 2001, the ITI has received the 'A' grade. In 2004, the institute was ranked second in the state of Maharashtra. In 2005 and 2006, the institute progressed to the first rank in the state. From 2006 till date, the institute has won the national-level Best Institute Award by the Central Government a total of seven times, and 21 trainees of the institute have ranked first in the state of Maharashtra, 12 students qualified for all-India level training and seven have bagged first rank at the national level. The first three toppers were felicitated by the state government with an award of Rs. 10,000/- each. The four subsequent toppers were honoured as 'Best Artisan of India' with an award of Rs. 50,000/- each by the Central Government. The credit for this achievement goes to the hard work of the talented students and the focused guidance given by dedicated teachers. These achievements have boosted everybody's enthusiasm.

□

25

Management of Hospitals

Take care of the patient and everything else will follow.

—Thomas First, M.D.[45]

As explained in the earlier chapter on education, a similar scenario exists in the field of healthcare. Healthcare is also becoming unaffordable for the common man and hence, there is a need for temples, NGOs and social institutions to attempt to provide affordable healthcare. Shri Sai Baba Sansthan Shirdi has entered the field of healthcare in the remote town of Shirdi and has occupied centrestage. Management of hospitals has become an essential part of temple management. Let us learn a lesson on healthcare from these hospitals.

Sai Baba's Emphasis on Healthcare[30]

Sai Baba cured many patients and freed them from the clutches of disease. Inspired by his example, two well-equipped hospitals with 575 beds, including a super speciality hospital, have been functioning in his memory at Shirdi for a number of years. There was a constant shortage of medicines. Medicines worth Rs. 66 crore were purchased to mitigate this shortage. Many of the machines at the hospital were over 15-years old. As many as 128 new machines, including Cath Lab, CT Scan and MRI machines were purchased at a cost of Rs.35 crore (Rs. 350 million). A number of medical camps were held besides modernising the hospitals. Shri Sainath Hospital was made entirely free of cost, starting from 1 January 2017. This is a small attempt to make readers aware of the existing medical facilities at Shirdi and the concerted attempts to modernise them.

Practical Application

Many theories float around the globe. Often, the proponents of these theories are themselves not serious about their practical application. A theory cannot be established unless it is proven that it can be put into practice. Theory alone is a lifeless entity and unless it is put into practice, it has little or no value. At Shri Sai Baba Sansthan, Shirdi, one can find actual examples of Sai's philosophy being implemented in the real world. Now that we are conversant with the Sai philosophy, we also need to know its practical application.

Feeding the hungry and serving patients was close to Baba's heart. The essence of his life was service. In addition to the *mantra* of *shraddha* (faith) and *saburi* (patience), Sai Baba advocated service, with a special emphasis on service of the poor, sick and ailing. He would lovingly care for patients. Even today, the eyes of Sai Baba idols or paintings manifest his compassion and maternal love. One loving glance from his eyes would suffice to relieve the pain of suffering devotees.

On reading *Shri Sai Satcharitra,* the story of Sai Baba's life, one learns about various incidents that reflect his deep concern for the sick. It is through Sai Baba's inspiration that Shirdi Sansthan now manages two hospitals at Shirdi. These hospitals are performing sterling service towards society.

Having access to well-equipped modern hospitals in a small town like Shirdi seemed impossible, but Sai Sansthan has successfully completed this task. A huge number of devotees visit Shirdi for *darshan*. The Sansthan has set up two hospitals for the benefit of the devotees as well as the residents of Shirdi and the country. Free or low-cost treatment, prompt service and compassion towards patients are the hallmarks of these hospitals.

Publicity by Word-of-mouth

I surveyed these hospitals and observed that they were equipped to offer excellent service with proper facilities. However, awareness about the medical facilities in Shirdi among the people was very low. Various efforts had to be taken to create this awareness. Along with it, we needed to further modernise the hospitals and equip them more fully. Latest equipment and ultra-modern machines for treatment were required. I decided to make this a priority by finding ways to purchase these machines. I also prepared a detailed plan for conducting various medical camps in order to make the common people aware of the medical facilities available. I attempted to publicise the medical camps among the poor and needy through extensive use of mass/social media. Word-of-mouth publicity by the patients, who received treatment, was the most effective. It had more impact because it came from first-hand experience of the patient who propagated the information about hospitals. This could be accomplished through the different programmes that were organised during the Sai Samadhi Centenary celebrations.

Free Medical Treatment

A record number of patients benefited from these camps. Another significant achievement was the Sainath Hospital at Shirdi, which started offering free-of-cost treatment from 1st January, 2017 and is one of its kind in India.

The two hospitals managed by the Sansthan have proudly kept the flag of medical service flying. They are renowned not only in the state of Maharashtra but in the entire country. Patients from various parts of India come to these hospitals for treatment. Sainath Hospital (with 325 beds) and Sai Baba Super Speciality Hospital (with 250 beds) treat around 5.5 lakh (0.55 million) patients every year. Sometimes, patients, who were refused admission or were asked to give up hope by renowned hospitals elsewhere, have come to Shirdi and have been miraculously cured. Through the medical treatment by the skilled doctors and the blessings of Sai Baba combined, the percentage of patients who recover is very high.

Sainath Hospital

The Sainath Hospital had a humble beginning as a dispensary in 1964. Today, it is a well-equipped hospital with 325 beds. General surgery, general medicine, paediatrics, gynaecology, orthopaedics, ENT, ophthalmology, dentistry, physiotherapy–all these facilities are offered here. Besides allopathy, homeopathic and Ayurvedic treatments are also provided. The healing touch that is full of care and compassion is a unique feature of the treatment carried out here. The doctors have introduced a number of innovative initiatives that have benefited thousands of patients. Internationally renowned doctors from all over the world specially participate in these initiatives.

Saibaba Hospital

The Sainath Hospital has an intensive care unit (ICU) with eight beds. From 1 January, 2017, all the treatments at this hospital have been offered free of cost. The patient is only required to pay Rs.10 for the initial case paper. This was a historic decision. Many patients from all over the country come to the hospital for treatment. Not only are the patients given free food, even their relatives are given free-of-cost meals from the *prasadalaya*. Residential arrangements for the patients' relatives are also made free of cost. The relatives are provided free transport in buses that ply between the hospitals and the residential buildings. Over and above, the patients are paid for a return ticket to their home town on getting discharged from the hospital.

Mobile Clinic

The Mobile Clinic and the First-Aid Centre at the Sai Mandir are seemingly simple services, but they have benefited a large number of patients. The Mobile Clinic consists of a well-equipped ambulance from the hospital that caters to around five to seven villages outside Shirdi. Every ambulance is equipped with a team comprising one doctor, one pharmacist, one staff nurse and one medical attendant. The ambulance halts at a predetermined place in every village. Patients from the village gather there; they are examined and given medicines on the spot and these are free of cost. Villagers who tend to ignore minor ailments and women who cannot find the time for medical treatment due to the burden of work are the main beneficiaries of this scheme.

First-Aid

The First-Aid Centre in the temple area is another apparently simple but very useful scheme. There are two such centres near the temple, and they offer their services from 6 a.m. to 11 p.m. every day. On festive days or heavily crowded days, first-aid is offered at six locations, including Bhakta Niwas and the *prasadalaya* (mess). The First-Aid Centres offer primary treatment to the devotees visiting Shirdi for *darshan*. The hospital administration has identified the needs of the devotees and found a creative way to fulfil them.

General Surgery

The General Surgery Department of the hospital has won special renown. It is staffed by skilled doctors, such as Dr. Ram Naik. He works unceasingly from 8 in the morning to 10 at night and has successfully performed complicated surgeries, such as pancreatic surgery. Dr. Ramdas Awhad has been working in the Ayurvedic department for the past 18 years without accepting remuneration of any kind. In the ophthalmology department, 20 to 25 cataract surgeries are performed daily, using the new phaco method.

A government centre for treatment of TB and AIDS has been set up in the hospital. The Sansthan has provided the space required for this centre.

Help to Underprivileged Patients

There are specific guidelines, following which poor and needy patients are given a grant of Rs. 25,000/-. This amount is handed over to the hospital where the patient receives further treatment. This scheme is being run since 1964. The scheme has now been revised to increase the grant to Rs. 50,000/-.

At present, 64 doctors are working at the hospital. There are eight visiting doctors. If we include the doctors who volunteer on special occasions, the number of doctors total around 100.

Skilled doctors, free of cost treatment and the compassionate care given by the hospital staff–these factors attract a large number of patients to these hospitals. The patients come not only from Maharashtra, but from all parts of the nation. Devotion towards Sai Baba also brings patients for treatment.

Medical Camps

An innovative project that was implemented was the organisation of special medical camps for various diseases during the Sai Samadhi Centenary celebrations. Seven special medical camps were organised during this year with very good response. One of the purposes of these camps was to spread awareness in the villages about the medical facilities in Shirdi.

The first medical camp was for an eye check-up. Thousands of patients were examined and given suitable spectacles. If suitable spectacles were not readily available for some patients, they were prepared and delivered to them after the camp. Mr. Prakash Gangavani gave special assistance for organising this camp. Dr. Saumil Kothari from Vision Eye Foundation, Mumbai, participated in the camp for cataract treatment. In two days, he and his team of colleagues performed 107 surgeries to remove cataract and correct strabismus.

In January 2018, a medical camp for the treatment of kidney stones was conducted. Dr. Ketan Shukla from Ahmedabad is a nationally renowned expert in this kind of surgery. He visits Shirdi hospital four to five times a year, bringing with him his own well-equipped medical van. He has successfully performed even the most complicated of surgeries.

The Jaipur Foot Camp (prosthetic leg) held in February can be called the crowning glory of our efforts. The Mumbai branch of Bhagwan Mahavir Vikalang Sahayata Samiti provided special assistance in organising it. During this six-day camp, 709 patients received treatment. Dr. D.R. Mehta, who has been honoured with Padma Bhushan and is the former chairman of SEBI, travelled from Jaipur to visit the camp. The 85-year-old Dr. Mehta personally spoke to every single patient who received treatment on the day of his visit. Not a single patient who participated in the camp was sent away without treatment. Some years ago, Dr. Mehta had become a victim of an accident in which he injured his leg. He was confined to bed for many days. He was distressed at imagining the plight of those who had lost their legs due to accidents. This distress led him to invent the Jaipur Foot, a prosthetic foot. Along with the Jaipur Foot Camp, a camp for prosthetic arms was also held. The Rotary Club of Pune Downtown gave special assistance for this camp, in which 74 patients were fitted with prosthetic arms.

Plastic surgery can be considered as one of the miracles in the field of medicine. A plastic surgery camp was conducted under the leadership of the well-known surgeon Dr. Ram Chilgar on behalf of the Aurangabad branch of the FIE Foundation. Nine expert doctors from countries, such as Taiwan, Singapore, Philippines, Peru and the USA visited Shirdi to participate in this camp. The world-renowned plastic surgeon from Taiwan, Dr. Hung Chi-Chen supervised the conduct of the camp. The 70-year-old Dr. Chen has developed a surgery for elephantiasis. He himself operated on a patient of elephantiasis in the camp. In the same camp, a very difficult operation on veins was successfully performed. Skin transplants were carried out on victims of burns. A total of 88 surgeries were performed during the three days of the camp, all free of cost. An ENT surgery and hearing aid distribution camp as well as a kidney stone treatment camp were held.

Modern Departments and Skilled Doctors

The hospitals are equipped with departments of cardiology, neurology, cardiac surgery, neurosurgery, orthopaedics, maxillofacial surgery, general medicine, general surgery, anaesthesiology, spine and joint, radiology, dental, paediatric surgery, onco-surgery, urology, plastic surgery, gastroenterology, dietetics, physiotherapy and chest physicians.

Sai Baba Super Speciality Hospital

In accordance with Sai Baba's teachings that the service to patients is service to God, the Sai Baba Super Speciality Hospital was set up by the Sansthan in 2006. The hospital has 250 beds and a large number of patients from Maharashtra as well as from other states are treated here.

Over the last 14 years, the hospital has acquired a highly positive reputation. I cherished the dream of making it a leading hospital in India by modernising it with the latest medical equipment and treatments. Whenever I went to Shirdi, visiting both the hospitals and conversing with the patients was a part of my routine. I would talk to the patients with concern and learn first-hand about their problems and difficulties. This knowledge helped me identify what steps could be taken to improve the facilities offered by the hospitals. One of the thrust areas I identified was the replacement of all the old machines with the latest ones with higher capacity. I got special grants sanctioned by the Board of Trustees of the Sansthan and the government of Maharashtra for the purchase of specific 128 machines. The purchase of foreign-manufactured machines was carried out as follows: CT scan: Rs. 6.74 crores (Rs. 67.4 million); MRI: Rs. 15.60 crores (Rs.156 million), Cath lab: Rs. 5.06 crores (Rs.50.6 million) and 2D Echo: Rs.0.73 crores (Rs.7.3 million). Within a short period of time, Shri Sai Baba Super Speciality Hospital had become renowned for the super-specialised treatment of heart diseases, brain diseases, diseases of the spine, kidney diseases, joint replacement etc., not only in the state, but all over India. Dr. Vijay Narode played a key role in modernisation of the hospital.

A majority of patients come from the districts surrounding Shirdi, while some patients come from other parts of the country, having heard of the reputation of the hospitals. Some notable cases are the successful heart surgeries performed on the four-year-old Kavya Ghule from Ambegaon, Pune district, and on the two-and-a- half-year-old Rudrambh Patil from Muktainagar, near Jalgaon. On an average, five to six heart surgeries are performed daily at the hospital.

Rates for Medical Tests and Treatment

The rates for treatment at Shri Sai Baba Hospital have been determined keeping in mind the poor and needy patients. The treatments here cost 30-40 per cent less than those at other hospitals. The most important aspect is that not a single patient is given poor treatment just to extract money, unlike what happens in many hospitals.

Mahatma Phule Jan Arogya Yojana (Mahatma Phule Health Care Scheme)

At present, the Maharashtra government's ambitious scheme–Mahatma Phule Jan Arogya Yojana (earlier known as Rajiv Gandhi Jeevandayee Jan Arogya Yojana) is being implemented at Shri Sai Baba Hospital. Recently Ayushman Bharat Yojana has also been implemented, under which patients from all over the nation can receive super-speciality treatment free of cost. Under this scheme, thousands of patients have received the benefit of free surgeries for different heart conditions.

The new scheme offers greater ease of access compared to the previous scheme. Applications under the scheme get approved within just two or three hours. As per the regulations governing the scheme, tests, surgery and treatment are conducted free of cost. Also, at the time of discharge, the patient is given sufficient medicines for 10 days and the fare to travel back to their native village in cash. The majority of patients and their families are satisfied with the treatment under this scheme.

Overall, the Mahatma Phule Jan Arogya Yojana is a blessing for patients and their families. It is also easy for the hospital management to implement. As a special grant, this scheme has been implemented by the Maharashtra state government at Shri Sai Baba Hospital, which is registered as a Referring Hospital. Once a patient is registered under this scheme, they receive free-of-cost treatment, right from making the case paper up to the surgery. Under this scheme, 43,993 outpatients have been treated free of cost till date. Similarly, 18,414 patients were admitted to the hospital for free-of-cost treatment.

According to a survey conducted by the Maharashtra state government under this scheme, the Shri Sai Baba Hospital is ranked first in Maharashtra for cardiology and cardiac surgery. Shri Sai Baba Hospital has treated 9,646 cases of cardiology and 8,979 cases of cardiac surgery and received grants of around Rs.13 crores (Rs.130 million) till date.

Free Dialysis

Shri Sai Baba Hospital offers treatment for dialysis, using the latest machines for the benefit of kidney patients. Till date, dialysis has been performed on approximately 24,628 patients. This dialysis facility is being offered completely free of cost at Shri Sai Baba Hospital from 1st January 2017. Five dialysis machines are currently operational and around 15 to 20 patients undergo dialysis every day. A separate dialysis machine is made available for jaundice patients.

Cath Lab

In 2006, the Catheterisation Lab Department was set up at Shri Sai Baba Hospital for treating patients with heart conditions. Till date, the Cath lab has performed procedures on 67,380 patients. The Cath lab machine, which was in use for 15 years, has been replaced with an ultra-modern one. It is manufactured by Shimadzu Corporation, Japan, and around 250 tests were conducted before the machine was installed in the hospital. New MRI and CT scan machines were also purchased for the hospital. To bring the technology up to the latest standards, 128 machines at the hospital were replaced with newer models. The previous machines were more than 15-years old and, in some cases, their depreciated value had dropped even below the maintenance costs. The decision to replace all the machines with new, latest models was a very revolutionary one. With the support from the Trustees, I was able to successfully implement this decision.

PM National Relief Fund (Pant Pradhan Rashtriya Sahayata Nidhi)

Shri Sai Baba Hospital has been registered under the PM National Relief Fund by the Central Government. The registration was carried out at the recommendation of the Ministry of Health and Family Welfare. The Sai Baba Hospital was recommended because of its proper medical facilities, highly qualified and skilled doctors and paramedical, nursing and administrative staff, the latest technology, low-cost treatment and various facilities to patients.

Free Treatment for Employees

With the approval of the managing committee, Shri Sai Baba Sansthan offers free-of-cost treatment to its permanent employees. Contractual employees can also avail this benefit based on their years of service. Free-of-cost medical treatment is provided to the students on the educational campuses of the Sansthan and the residents of Shri Dwarkamai Old Age Home, Upasani Maharaj Kanya Kumari Ashram, Mahanubhav Ashram and Samvatsar. Victims of dog and snake bites are given injections free of cost, and patients of haemophilia from Ahmednagar district also receive free injections. Free-of-cost medical treatment is provided as required to the devotees who visit Shirdi for *darshan*.

Free Diagnostic Camps

Free diagnostic camps are conducted in remote villages of Maharashtra that do not have access to medical facilities.

Patients who require surgery or further treatment are identified and invited to Shirdi.

Waivers in Medical Bill Payments

Under the Bombay Public Trust Act 1950 and the provisions of the scheme as per the High Court, 10 per cent of patients below the poverty line shall be treated free of cost at hospitals. A monthly report of the same is submitted to the Charity Commissioner, Maharashtra state, Mumbai, and the Assistant Charity Commissioner, Ahmednagar. This department also provides guidance to patients and their families from time to time.

Honouring the Girl Child

One touching initiative by the hospital needs to be specially highlighted. Around 50 women deliver babies at the hospital every month. Mr. Rajendra Kote, chairman of Shiladhi Pratishthan, and Mr. Tushar Shelke, vice chairman, started a unique initiative to promote the 'Save the Girl Child' movement. Every girl child born in the hospital during the Centenary Year was honoured with the gift of a silver coin. Every mother who gave birth to a girl child was felicitated in a touching ceremony attended by doctors and nurses. This unique expression of care and concern stands testimony to the social responsibility and respect for women shown by Shiladhi Pratishthan and the hospital staff.

Free Thalassemia Treatment

A very touching advertisement about thalassemia used to be shown on television. It features a young girl suffering from thalassemia. She thanks most of the people she meets. On being asked why, she replies, "I am a patient of thalassemia. I need to undergo blood transfusions very often. I think that you might be someone who donated blood to me. So, I thank everyone." On hearing this, a touched and somewhat baffled man replies, "But child, I have never donated blood to you." The girl replies, "That's ok. Maybe you haven't, but you can keep my thanks for when you donate blood in future. Well, I must go and thank many others now." This advertisement had a strong emotional impact on me. I sincerely felt that the hospitals at Shirdi should give treatment for thalassemia too. I discussed it with the hospital authorities. They took planned efforts and hospitals started giving treatment for this incurable disease.

Thalassemia is a genetic disorder. Due to it, the creation of haemoglobin in the body slows down. The symptoms of this disease manifest within three months. The amount of blood in the body of the patient gets reduced and the patient requires frequent blood transfusions. As per the WHO, around 7,000-10,000 babies born in India every year suffer from thalassemia. At present, around 10 lakh babies in India are affected by thalassemia. Such patients are given free blood transfusions by the Shri Sainath Blood Bank.

Record Number of Cardiac Surgeries

Shri Sai Baba had a special concern for the sick and ailing. The Shri Sai Baba Hospital was started in order to carry forward Sai Baba's teachings of service to patients and the hospital has progressed rapidly. In the year 2007, a total of 1,300 cardiac surgeries were performed at the hospital. A special mention must be made of the 47 cardiac surgeries performed in 24 hours from 24 February 2007 to 25 February 2007. These 47 surgeries set a new world record. The surgeries were performed under the leadership of Dr. Aniruddha Dharmadhikari. This achievement was recorded in the *Guinness Book* and the *Limca Book of World Records*.

The percentage cure rate of patients is very high due to the *dava* (medicine) of the doctors and the *dua* (blessings) of Shri Sai Baba. Such a good healthcare facility in the remote place of Shirdi is the pride of the town. Management of hospitals by the temple is the most important part of temple management. The devotees continuously monitor the temple expenditure. When they find that a major portion of what they have donated is being used for the care of the needy and poor, they are satisfied and are inclined to donate more.

□

26

Management of Other Social Initiatives

We make a living by what we get.
We make a life by what we give.

—Unknown[46]

You have to give shape, direction and face to the society otherwise it will be just a crowd. You have to inculcate the spirit of social service. Normally, good sense prevails but you need to strengthen it. Slow and steady should be the approach. With this, all the temples could have a social outlook and could be oriented towards society. I introduced many social welfare initiatives in Shirdi, four of which are discussed here. The first of them was blood donation.

a. Blood Donation [30]

Like hair donation at Tirupathi or worship of God by offering leaves, flowers, fruits, milk and water, devotees are encouraged to donate blood. My vision was to bring about a unique blend of *shraddha* and service at Shirdi. Devotees visiting Tirupati for *darshan* donate their hair. I was confident that if we appealed to devotees at Shirdi to donate blood, it would create a massive blood donation movement. I rapidly devised a scheme and this vision became a reality

Requirement of Blood

A study by the National AIDS Control Organisation carried out in India in the year 2018 estimated a population need of 26.4 million units of blood, which implies that the country needs to collect 26.4 million units of whole blood to address the need for whole blood and components in the country. The clinical demand in healthcare facilities across the country was estimated to be 14.6 million units of blood. According to the study, the supply was found to be 13.5 million units in 2018; however, the annual collection reported by NACO in the country was 11.1 million units in 2017. Hence, although the country might collect nearly an adequate volume of blood in terms of overall country requirement, the distribution of availability and therefore, access, was not equitable.

In India, a lot of donated blood is wasted due to poor infrastructure and lack of storage facilities. The WHO recommends that for every 1,000 people in the country, around 10 donors are needed to provide an adequate supply of blood. Thus, around 1 per cent of the population must be targeted to serve as voluntary blood donors. There are a lot of misconceptions about blood donation, mostly due to lack of proper education and social atmosphere. It has been reported that the myths about blood donation are a major hurdle in blood collection.

Social Orientation

I had always cherished the vision that temples and places of pilgrimage should become more socially-oriented and service-oriented. I dreamed of creating a state-wide blood donation campaign at Shirdi, to manifest devotion in the form of social service. With everyone's cooperation, I was able to convert this dream into reality.

Every year, India celebrates National Voluntary Blood Donation Day on 1st October to highlight the need and importance of safe blood in the life of an individual. The WHO estimates that blood donation by one per cent of the population is generally the minimum to meet a nation's most basic need for blood. Even by this low measure, as per data presented to the Lok Sabha on 23 March, 2018, India was short of 1.9 million units of blood (or 15 per cent) vis-a-vis the WHO norm. In India, the concept of blood donation has always been demand-led, wherein even the most well-educated people perceive blood donation as an emergency service to be provided only when there is a need. Currently, most blood banks and hospitals in India are highly dependent on replacement blood donations, wherein family or friends are asked to donate blood in lieu of the units given to a patient. As a result, they are rarely able to maintain an adequate stock of different blood groups to meet the transfusion needs of all their patients, particularly in emergency situations. In addition, this puts constant pressure on patients to find blood donors in order to receive treatment.

In most aspects of healthcare, the availability of a service should precede its need. The same goes for blood. In a scenario where blood needs to be arranged to meet its need, there are risks of delays in surgical procedures, inadequate time to properly test the donor blood or effectively screen potential donors. Moreover, even some basic procedures, such as childbirth are accompanied by risk of haemorrhage, for which an ample stock of blood is required. Even today, in many remote areas, pregnant women are forced to travel to distant hospitals to deliver their child because the primary healthcare centres closest to them do not have sufficient blood available.

Need of Awareness

This cultural apathy of donating-as-directed coupled with widespread misinformation and ignorance about the effect, importance and safety of voluntary blood donation significantly impacts India's blood transfusion system by making it inefficient and disorganised. Awareness needs to be increased on voluntary blood donation for this behavioral change to happen. Building a chain of voluntary blood donors who regularly donate blood allows a consistent and reliable supply of safe blood when required and becomes more cost-effective than recruiting new donors. Through voluntary blood donation, patients have improved access to safe blood transfusion as the blood and blood products they receive carry a low risk of infection that might further compromise their health.

Voluntary Blood Donation

Voluntary blood donation programmes succeed only when people are well-aware of the sense of sacrifice behind it and are motivated by altruism and the desire to help others in need as a sense of moral duty or social responsibility. Therefore, it is important that we start inculcating this mindset change in India, to build awareness and behavioural change towards voluntary blood donation.

One of the most crucial challenges that affect blood availability in India is the inadequacy of repeat voluntary blood donors. The year 2019 promised to be the year of advancement in the Indian healthcare sector with Prime Minister Modi underscoring that a healthy life is the right of every person and giving a huge thrust to accessibility and affordability of healthcare services in India.

Campaign

Shirdi Devasthan is known across the world today. Sai devotees from all corners of the world and of India devoutly visit Shirdi for Sai Baba's *darshan*. It is said that 'at Shirdi, the devotion of Shegaon and the wealth of Tirupati is united'.

The revered Sai Baba not only preached *shraddha* (faith) and *saburi* (patience) to his devotees, he also advocated social service. Inspired by his ideals, I proposed the initiative of blood donation, an apparently simple yet extremely crucial service to society. I was confident that once the Sai devotees were made aware about the importance of blood donation and given suitable facilities for the same, they would respond to our appeal. For them, the act of blood donation would become the act of offering their most valuable possession to Sai Baba. Thus, I introduced the innovative campaign titled '*Tirupati mein keshdaan, Shirdi mein raktadaan*', which means 'Like hair donation at Tirupati, blood donation at Shirdi'. Devotees who visit Tirupati take great pride in donating their hair. The Sansthan appealed to Sai devotees to donate blood with the same sense of pride and sacrifice.

An average of 50,000 devotees visit Shirdi daily for Sai *darshan*. If we were able to convince them of the importance of blood donation, and, if even one per cent of the visitors donated blood, we would still collect 500 units of blood every day.

Appeal for Blood Donation

The Sai Baba Sansthan put up banners appealing for blood donation in the temple premises. A blood collection facility was set up in the temple premises, and this was the beginning of a *mahayadnya*–a mega campaign of blood donation. Initially, the response was small, but it started growing. Later, it reached a point where we were forced to say, "Please do not donate blood as our capacity for storage is exhausted." In the Trustee meeting, we came up with a solution for this problem. We decided to tie up with the blood banks of government institutions and NGOs. Initially, we appealed to a few blood banks to collect blood from Shirdi. Eventually, around 25 blood banks became associated with this blood donation campaign. At present, an average of 150-200 persons donate blood daily. In the Samadhi Centenary year of Sai Baba, the Sansthan collected around 50,000 units of blood. Though this is highly creditable, it does not constitute even one per cent of the devotees. The number can be increased so as to collect 500 units of blood daily–that is the ultimate target.

Shirdi Blood Bank

In the year 2000, a blood bank was set up at Shirdi. Rather than making devotees come to the blood bank, we wanted the blood bank to reach the devotees. So, the blood donation facility was set up in the temple premises itself. In 2004, a well-equipped centre for collecting blood was started. The then hon'ble Chief Minister Vilasrao Deshmukh inaugurated this campaign. Initially, blood donation facilities were available on two days in a week. At present, blood is collected on all seven days of the week. We decided to inscribe this in the minds of the devotees: 'just as you come to Shirdi for *darshan* of Sai Baba, you must also donate blood'. The donors are awarded with a certificate and honoured with a direct *darshan* of Sai Baba. This has helped promote the blood donation campaign and has boosted the enthusiasm of blood donors.

There are more than 8,000 Sai temples all over India and around 450 Sai temples in other countries. We have suggested to all that this blood donation movement should be run at all these temples. Thursday is an especially sacred day for Sai Baba, so I have appealed to Sai devotees to donate blood on Thursday.

I believe that blood donation by devotees during the Centenary Year celebrations was a significant public service. The success of this project convinced me that it must have been blessed by Sai Baba himself. I hope that the story of this initiative will provide inspiration to many other institutions.

If service is imbued with devotion, it reaches the feet of the Almighty. From this thought was born my idea of appealing to the devotees visiting Shirdi to donate blood. In a short time, this idea became a mega campaign.

The blood donated by Sai devotees is provided free of cost to the patients at Sainath Hospital. It is also provided free of cost to patients of Sai Baba Hospital admitted under the Mahatma Phule Scheme.

Mega Camp

During the Sai Baba Samadhi Centenary Year, the Sansthan

organised a mega blood donation camp. It was held on 30th December, 2017 and more than 1,000 units of blood were collected in this camp. Around 22 blood banks participated in this initiative.

The blood donation movement is managed very well by Dr. Maithili Pitambare of Sainath Hospital.

Component Analysis

The blood bank at the Sansthan has the advanced equipment required to carry out the analysis and component separation of the blood collected. One unit of blood benefits three patients. Dr. Suryakant Patil ably manages this department with his team of 24 colleagues. In 2017, the blood bank collected 16,000 units of blood. We are rapidly advancing towards making Sai Sansthan the largest blood donation centre in the entire state. I am sure that this seed of blood donation will spread to all the temples and it will become a national movement of blood donation.

If each of us understands the importance of blood donation and the saying 'Blood donor of today may be a blood receiver tomorrow', we shall never face a shortage of blood. The Sansthan is thus making comprehensive efforts to fulfil its social responsibility. The lion's share of the credit for the successful campaign goes to the employees of the blood bank. It is always energising to meet them.

It may be noted that there is no alternative to human blood. Efforts to create artificial blood by scientists have not been fully successful, though partial success has been achieved. The blood so created cannot perform all the functions of natural blood, but it can do so to a limited extent.

This shows the importance of temple management as a social movement.

b. Sai Agarbatti

Refuse what you do not need; reduce what you do need; reuse what you consume; recycle what you cannot refuse, reduce, or reuse; and rot (compost) the rest.

—Bea Johnson[47]

Sai *agarbatti* (incense) is yet another important social initiative. It is the miracle creating wealth out of waste. All medium to big temples can adopt it and get the benefits.

200 Local Women Empowered[30]

The flowers offered to Sai Baba by devotees used to be thrown away as waste. I conceived the idea of recycling these floral offerings into incense sticks. This was an eco-friendly concept and through the fragrance of the incense sticks, devotees would be able to delight in Baba's presence for a longer time. The resulting Agarbatti Project has given employment to 200 needy local women and has an annual turnover of Rs. 5 crores (Rs. 50 million).

Devotion is a special feature of the Indian mindset. No other country can boast of such a huge population that is devoted to its deities. Sai Baba commands the devotion of crores of people, and lakhs of devotees have experienced the grace of his blessings. Devotion to Sai Baba is growing day by day.

As Sai Baba was very fond of flowers, almost every devotee offers garlands or a bunch of flowers to Baba as part of their worship. The quantity of floral offerings is very high on Thursdays, Sundays and festive days. The sheer scale of these offerings is awe-inspiring, but, on the other hand, it creates the problem of disposing of these flowers.

After becoming the chairman of the Trust, I took a stroll through the temple premises. I approached Baba's *samadhi* through the *darshan* queue. Devotees were offering garlands, bouquets and flowers to Baba's idol and at the *samadhi*. I wondered what happened to these flowers later. I returned to my office, but this question continued to preoccupy me.

Flowers Thrown in Garbage

On inquiring, I learned that around three-and-a-half tonnes of flowers are offered to Baba daily. On Thursdays, Sundays and festive days, the quantity of flowers offered goes up to even four tonnes. I was shocked to hear how these flowers were disposed of: they were simply thrown away as waste. It was impossible to reconcile this with my beliefs and values and really disturbed me. Since these flowers represent the feelings and devotion of the devotees, I could not wrap my head around the idea of them being thrown away as waste. Then I realised that the flowers offered to Baba could be recycled into fragrant *agarbattis* or incense sticks.

Stop Offering Flowers

Before arriving at the production of *agarbattis*, a proposal was forcefully raised to stop floral offerings in the temple. In this process, it was revealed that hundreds of farmers from around 50 adjoining villages were involved in producing these flowers, and hundreds of people were employed in making garlands and bouquets and hundreds of them were involved in selling them to the devotees. If the flowers were not allowed in the temple, it would render thousands of people jobless. Therefore, the suggestion was not accepted by the Sansthan and floral offerings continued as before.

Upcycling Flowers into *Agarbatti*

I invited representatives from various organisations that produced *agarbattis* to discuss this issue. From among them, we selected the organisation named Eco Nirmiti Foundation. It was resolved that the Sansthan would provide floral offerings to Eco Nirmiti and that the transport arrangements for the same would be made by them. The organisation would then separate the flower petals, dry them, turn them into powder and produce *agarbattis* by applying glue to this powder. Eco Nirmiti started this work and 200 local women in need of work were employed under this project. Per day, they produced 5,000 packets containing 30 *agarbattis* each. Each packet is sold for Rs.30/-. This amounts to a daily income of Rs. 1.5 lakhs (Rs. 0.15 million), which makes an annual turnover of around Rs. 5 crores (Rs. 50 million). The Sansthan also benefits from the project because 10 per cent of the proceeds amounting to Rs.50 lakhs (Rs. 5 million) are given to the Sansthan as per the agreement with Eco Nirmiti. Besides, the *agarbattis* also have emotional value for the devotees. They believe that these *agarbattis* carry the presence of Baba and the fragrance of devotion. As they also create wealth, these *agarbattis* not only carry the fragrance of devotion, they also inspire respect.

Essence, *Dhoop*, *Gulkand*

In the future, essence, *dhoop* and *gulkand* can also be produced by recycling these flowers. The stems and leaves of the flowers are converted into fertiliser. In order to reach out to devotees with these *agarbattis*, the Sansthan has given Eco Nirmiti a room counter to sell them. These *agarbattis* have been received enthusiastically by the devotees. They take pride in gifting them to their near and dear ones.

Earlier, due to a lack of other options, the Sansthan was forced to dump the daily floral offerings as waste at the local municipal dumping ground. We resolved to find a sustainable and long-term solution to this problem. With the cooperation of Eco Nirmiti (now Janaseva Foundation) and the involvement of women belonging to self-help groups, we set up this project of recycling the waste floral offerings into *agarbattis*. This is a unique project that not only ensures the cleanliness of the temple premises, but also respects the feelings of devotees and infuses the entire atmosphere with devotion.

The Project

This project involves various tasks, such as collecting the floral offerings from the temple, transporting them to the plant, classifying the flowers, separating the rose petals, drying them and grinding them into a powder and turning it into *agarbattis* that give out a soft fragrance.

Ordinary enterprises are quite commonly set up. What is unique about this project is its orientation towards public service. A maximum number of women have been employed in this project. The task of collecting floral offerings from the temple has been assigned entirely to women employees. Thirty women employees work in shifts to ensure that this work is done on all seven days of the week. As women employees are more effective at canvassing the devotees about this project, which aims at cleanliness and at creating a new product, this task is given to them. The company has deployed two vehicles to transport the floral offerings to the plant.

The floral offerings to Sai Baba mostly consist of roses, zendu and *sabja* flowers. At present, the rose petals are used for manufacturing *agarbattis*, which are marketed under the name 'Sai Dwarakamai'. The other flowers are converted into a manure used for the Sansthan's gardens. But in future, *agarbattis* will be produced from all these flowers.

The story of this startup enterprise tells us the importance of temple management and their potential for creating a business enterprise.

c. Sai Sevak

Successful people are always looking for opportunities to help others.
Unsuccessful people are always asking, 'What's in it for me?

—Brian Tracy[48]

Even after I had taken charge as the chairman, the experience in the *darshan* queue kept nagging at my mind. I had returned without taking *darshan*, feeling humiliated. I started my duties with the memory of the humiliation fresh in my mind. I resolved to tackle the inconvenience faced by the thousands of devotees visiting Shirdi daily. My service to Sai would be meaningful only if I could complete this one task.

Unique Manifestation of Devotion[30]

We have a tradition of seeing God in the form of His devotees. When we bow down to a *waarkari* (one who walks from home to Pandharpur and back), who has returned from Pandharpur, we gain the satisfaction of having bowed down to Vitthal himself. Gadge Maharaj went to Pandharpur a number of times and constructed a *dharmashala* (free accommodation) and a *ghaat* (wharf) for devotees. But he never entered the temple. He believed that service to devotees was the best worship of the Lord. I decided to implement an innovative concept–the Sai Sevak Scheme–where devotees could take care of other devotees, so that the devotees visiting Shirdi received proper facilities and hassle-free *darshan*.

Apace with the rapid progress of science and technology in India, faith in God is growing. As a result, places of worship have record numbers of visiting devotees on festive occasions, and even on ordinary days. Vaishnodevi, Tirupati, Padmanabh Mandir, Rameshwar, Madurai, Mantralaya, Dharmasthal, Siddhivinayak Mandir, Shani Shingnapur, Gajanan Maharaj

Mandir-Shegaon, and other temples are witnessing this phenomenon. Shirdi, which is a beloved destination of people, not only in India but all over the world, attracts a growing number of devotees. An average of 50,000-70,000 devotees per day visit the Shirdi *Sai Mandir* for *darshan*. On many days of the month, the number crosses one lakh. On festive days, such as Ram Navami, Guru Purnima or Dussehra, the number of visiting devotees exceeds three lakhs. The trustees and the administration of Shirdi Sansthan strive continuously to ensure that all the devotees receive proper *darshan* of their God. Lodging and meals also need to be provided for devotees coming from far-off places.

Innovative Scheme

I chalked out an innovative scheme named *Sai sevak* to implement crowd management and control, maintain discipline and ensure the comfort of devotees. Very soon, the *Sai sevak* scheme became a special feature of the Sansthan.

Being a scientist, I always insist that every task must be done with discipline and precision. Rather than bringing in outsiders to manage the *darshan* crowd and to provide various facilities, I wanted to accomplish it through self-motivated devotee participation.

I was aware that an innovative system of service by volunteers was run at Gajanan Maharaj Mandir, Shegaon. I visited Shegaon myself to learn about this system. Shiv Shankar Bhau Patil, chairman of the Gajanan Maharaj Mandir Sansthan, helped me understand the working of this system. Shiv Shankar Bhau had some reservations about whether a similar system would work in Shirdi, but I was determined. I told him to give me his blessings and I would do it successfully. We decided to implement this system and the devotees gave us an overwhelming response.

The number of devotees visiting Shirdi is very large when

compared to those visiting Shegaon. Managing the diverse crowd from across India and 43 countries and providing them with various facilities in an organised manner is a huge challenge. The volunteers under the *Sai sevak* scheme of the Sansthan devotedly fulfil these responsibilities.

Meticulous Planning

The scheme has been meticulously planned to run uninterrupted all year round. Ten groups of 21 volunteers each are selected for service every week. So, a total of 210 *Sai sevaks* work throughout the week. The week of service begins on Tuesday and concludes on the following Monday. The volunteers work in shifts from 6 a.m. to 2 p.m .and from 2 p.m. to 10 p.m. and they go about their duties joyfully, chanting 'Om Sai Ram'. *Palkhi mandals*–those who carry Sai Baba's palanquin every year on their shoulders to Shirdi–have been permitted to register more than one group of volunteers per week, and groups are allowed to perform service for more than one week, if they so desire. The members of various *palkhi mandals* are given priority as *Sai sevaks* because they have an understanding of hardship, which they experience during their *palkhi yatra*. Members of such *mandals* can create a group of at least 21 volunteers and register themselves with the Sansthan.

Overwhelming Response

With 10 groups every week, we wanted 520 groups to register over the year, but the response to the scheme was so overwhelming that on the very first day, 570 groups got registered, thus making it a full house on the very first day.

The *Sai sevaks* in every group are allotted specific duties. They happily undertake the service, whether it is applying *gandha tilak* to devotees' foreheads, serving water, distributing *prasad*, cutting vegetables, serving meals, giving information at stalls or helping patients at the hospital.

The Sanstha provides certain facilities for the *Sai sevaks* to be able to work efficiently. The *sevaks* are issued an identity card by the Sansthan and are given a uniform to be worn during volunteer service. They are provided free-of-cost accommodation, breakfast and meals by the Sansthan. If a *Sai sevak* falls ill during this voluntary service, he is given free treatment at the Sansthan hospitals.

Rules and Regulations

At the same time, the Sansthan has also defined certain rules for *Sai sevaks*. Shri Suryabhan Game played a key role in the design and implementation of this system. Any volunteer, who broke these rules or misbehaved in any way, was immediately relieved from volunteer duties. The *Sai sevaks* can work only in the allotted departments and are not allowed to select the kind of duty they want to perform. The system is so well-organised that by rotation everyone gets to serve in various places, including one day in the *Samadhi Mandir*. On completing their week of volunteer work, the *sevaks* must return their uniform, service card and identity card to the Sansthan. The rules also state that a police complaint will be registered against any *Sai sevak* found to be committing fraud or promoting superstition.

At first, police verification was made mandatory before registering a *Sai sevak*. While this rule has been relaxed, however, an affidavit from the chief of the concerned *palkhi mandal* is required.

The *Sai sevak* scheme received an overwhelming response, since every devotee yearns to serve Sai. It created a record of sorts. The remarkable feature is that these volunteers do not get remuneration in any form, except for free-of-cost lodging and board. The largest number of *Sai sevaks* come from Andhra Pradesh. As many as 250 groups comprising 5,300 volunteers from Andhra have rendered service to Sai. Maharashtra ranks second, with 188 groups comprising 3,619 volunteers. Groups of *Sai sevaks* come from West Bengal, Tamil Nadu, Kerala and Uttarakhand as well. Some groups of volunteers have even travelled from other countries, such as Malaysia, Dubai and Oman.

The devotees coming for being asked to manage the other devotees is a fine example of community participation. I appealed to the devotees: 'Just as we see Lord Vitthal in a waarkari from Pandharpur, we can serve Sai in the form of devotees coming for Sai *darshan*.'

Oath

Sai sevaks need to have moral rules to govern their conduct. We formulated an oath which is to be sworn by every Sai Sevak before commencing their duties. The oath is as follows:

I hereby swear that...

I (name) swear in the name of Shri Sai Baba that, as a Sai sevak*:*

- *I shall always practise cleanliness*
- *I shall always refrain from any addiction*
- *I shall not indulge in any misbehaviour*
- *I shall always strive to eradicate superstition*
- *I shall always follow Shri Sai Baba's mantra of shraddha and saburi*
- *I shall serve everyone with complete devotion*
- *I shall behave humbly and politely with everyone*
- *I shall uphold the respect of the post of* Sai sevak *with mind, body and speech.*

Om Sai Ram!

Sai Sevak–A Responsibility

At the inauguration of the *Sai sevak* scheme, I expressed the thought behind the concept. I told the volunteers, "The post you will occupy is a unique one. You have not attained it through any form of competition. You must bear in mind that by selecting you for service, Baba has given you a huge opportunity. You have been selected because of Baba's love for you. The seven days you spend here will be only a starting point of your service. You have willingly accepted the mantle of service and should humbly bear it throughout your lives. The concept of *Sai sevak* carries a special meaning. There are many employees who work at the Sansthan, but you are *sevaks* (volunteers). There is a distinction between work and service, just as there is a difference between water and *teertha*. Scientifically, both are water and can be represented as H_2O; however, they differ in their significance. When water is imbued with devotion, it becomes *teertha*. Similarly, when work is performed with devotion, it becomes service."

Unique feature of the *Sai sevak* scheme

Another unique feature of the *Sai sevak* scheme is the accidental insurance scheme coverage provided. The Sansthan obtains an accidental insurance cover of one lakh rupees for every volunteer who completes one week of service as a *Sai sevak*. This facility was started from 17 July 2018, and *Sai sevaks* have been awarded the insurance certificates.

Every service matters, irrespective of how small the task may be. *Teertha* is consumed in a small spoonful–no one asks for a glass full of *teertha*, but that small spoonful of *teertha* is sufficient to purify the full body and mind. The same goes for service. A small amount of service can achieve what remains unattainable through tonnes of work. You must perform your service with this devoted mindset.

Launch on Guru Purnima

The *Sai sevak* scheme was launched on Guru Purnima, 29th July, 2017. The scheme has been functioning continuously and with undiminished enthusiasm ever since. Volunteer devotees take up duties at the *darshan* queue, the *prasadalaya*, sale of *prasad ladoos*, security, restaurant, *bhakta-niwas* and the hospital.

Certificate in appreciation of service

The Sansthan implemented a number of innovative concepts under the *Sai sevak* scheme. A common ceremony is held to welcome the new groups of volunteers and to bid farewell to the groups who have completed their service. The volunteers who have completed service share their experiences and the senior employees of the Sansthan provide guidance to the new volunteers. Certificates of completion of service are awarded and the new volunteers are administered the oath.

□

27

Sai Sangam, Shirdi

When there is no enemy within, the enemies outside cannot hurt you.

—Winston S. Churchill[49]

Let us now discuss the fourth and innovative initiative that happened for the first time in the history of Sai Sansthan.

Devotion to Sai Baba Transcended National Borders[30]

There are many Sai temples in India and abroad. I envisioned a network that would bring together all these Sai temples. I expressed a desire that Sai temples all over the world should work for society with a common aim to promote social responsibility in all their activities. To accomplish this, we organised two international conferences at Shirdi for the trustees of Sai temples drawn from all over the world. Both were well attended, with the participation of Sai devotees from 22 countries. Hon'ble Venkaiah Naidu, Vice President of India, addressed the conference.

Sai Temples in 43 Countries

The family of Sai devotees is the largest group of devotees in the world. No other modern saint has so many temples built in his honour all over the world. There are more than

450 Sai temples in countries other than India. The USA alone has 80 Sai temples, Malaysia 22, the UK five and so on. A total of 43 countries, such as Germany, France, Japan, Australia, New Zealand and Switzerland have Sai temples and there are around 8,000 Sai temples in India. Nearly half of these are located in Andhra Pradesh and Telangana. It is to be noted that these are considerably large Sai temples. Thus, the Sai movement is international. These temples have a number of common features. Therefore, I desired that there should be a common association of all the Sai temples and that they should coordinate their activities.

Social Orientation

I aimed at making these temples more oriented towards the devotees and towards service to society. With this aim, we organised the first international conference of the Sai temple Trustees from all over India and the world on 11th and 12th December, 2016 at Shirdi. The conference received an enthusiastic response. On 23rd December, 2017, the second international conference of *Sai Mandir* Trustees was also successfully organised in the *Sai Mandir* premises. Hon'ble Vice President of India, Shri Venkaiah Naidu, graced the occasion with his presence. These conferences were attended by 4,000 trustees of around 1,028 Sai temples from 24 states of India and from 22 countries.

Aims and Objects

While addressing the participants, I explained the rationale behind my idea of organising the conference. This international conference of *Sai Mandir* Trustees was probably the first effort of its kind. We deliberated on how to create coordination between various temples and how to make their initiatives more oriented towards service to society. We also exchanged ideas on planning and implementation of common initiatives across the world. The five initiatives–blood donation, educational activities, healthcare services, organ donation and food donation–were resolved as mandatory for the temples.

We also announced five additional activities, which can be taken up, depending on local needs–eradication of illiteracy, poverty alleviation, removal of superstitions, organising yoga camps and environmental initiatives. We also resolved to maintain basic uniformity in the *poojas* and *aartis* performed. I am happy to share that the Sai temple at Shirdi has been awarded the ISO certification. The detailed rituals of the *pooja* and *aartis* performed at Shirdi temple and the details of the *prasad* are easily available on the temple website. People can use them to ensure that uniform *pooja* rituals are performed in all the *Sai Mandirs*.

Another aim of the conference was to connect all the Sai temples in the world with the main temple at Shirdi, which is the powerhouse for all these temples and trustees. Shirdi is a holy *sangam* place, just like Prayag-*teertha* (a confluence of the holy rivers Ganga, Yamuna and Saraswati) in India or the Vatican in Europe, for all the Sai temples.

Largest Movement

It was wonderful to listen to Shri Venkaiah Naidu speak to the audience in five languages–Sanskrit, Telugu, Hindi, English and Marathi. His words touched the people's hearts. He spoke spontaneously and did not deliver a written speech like most dignitaries. He touched the hearts because he was speaking from the heart. The audience was immersed in his speech.

I believe that the family of Sai devotees is the largest group of its kind in the world. No other movement has so many followers. When I reflected on who was the founder of this huge movement, I realised that there is no defined leader for this immense family. There is no single person who has travelled all over India and the world to establish Sai temples. Also, no one travelled from Shirdi to all these places with the aim of establishing temples. Therefore, one has to conclude that the mover and promoter of this immense movement is none other than Sai Baba himself. Various devotees had divine experiences of Sai Baba and were motivated to establish Sai temples. The number of temples began to increase and they became popular of their own accord. We believed that this movement across the world should become more organised and should have a proper management.

Lead by Example

Sai Baba has taught us by leading himself in the service to society. If we want to worship Sai Baba, we must do it through the act of social service, which he would like most.

I am confident that, through the efforts of *Sai sevaks*, Sai devotees and Sai temples, no resident of the respective locality will go hungry and everyone will have access to education and healthcare services. Through these initiatives, the Sai devotee movement will touch the hearts of the people. I envision that all the Sai temples in the world will join this movement.

The conference was highly successful. It was my sincere effort to bring together the Sai temples from all over the world. The response we received was overwhelming. Participants expressed their satisfaction, saying that they had been coming to Shirdi all these years, but this time Baba had called them to Shirdi. It was a memorable event which people would cherish for a long time.

It is just an indication of the positive influence the temple management can have on the society. It can change the perception of people about the temple; the temple does not remain just a building or deity but becomes a living entity.

□

28

Looking Forward

The journey of a thousand miles begins with one step.

—Lao Tzu[50]

I am confident that a number of temples will find the subject of temple management a very useful one. I look forward to interaction with temples, religious institutions, organisers of spiritual tourism, temple architects, institutions and all those who are interested in the subject of temple management from the professional perspective. The temples have a great employment potential which has not been harnessed so far. Wealth of the temples together is very large. People are generally religious; one doesn't need to invite people to visit the temple. It happens through auto route. There is a good amount of following for the temples. Therefore the temples could be the mover of social change or transformation of the society. The basic need is that they should be professionally managed. With this, the society and the temples would be the ultimate beneficiaries because discipline and organisation will get inculcated in the temples. The ultimate aim should be to provide a satisfactory spiritual *darshan* experience to the devotees.

Educational institutions could take a lead in creating

the type of manpower that is required by the temples by instituting professional training. With the emergence of trained professionals in temple management, a new market will open up. This will generate qualified manpower, which, I am sure, will be welcomed by the temples in India.

I do not claim to have presented the subject of temple management in a complete manner. There would always be the supplementary and complementary trades to find a place in the subject. With evolution, this will achieve completeness. This would take some time, but it is important to initiate discussion and academic deliberation on it. The book is a good starting point. There should be deliberations and workshops organised in temples and institutions on the subject of temple management involving the professionals. They are capable of value addition to the subject.

I look forward to such interaction.

Om Sai Ram!!!

□

References

1. https://www.brainyquote.com/quotes/john_c_maxwell_383606
2. https://www.brainyquote.com/authors/lee-iacocca-quotes
3. https://blog.vantagecircle.com/management-quotes/
4. https://www.azquotes.com/author/2886-Winston_Churchill/tag/planning
5. https://quotefancy.com/quote/1608954/
6. Erik van Vulpen, AIRH digital, seven human resource management basics every HR professional should know, digitalhrtech.com
7. https://www,goodreads.com/quotes/18976
8. https://www.brainyquote.com/quotes/swami_vivekananda_557617
9. Lumen, Boundless Management, https://courses.lumenlearning.com/boundless- management/chapter/decision-making-in-management/
10. https://www.pinterest.com/pin/350295677251407764/
11. Henrico Dolfing, Strategy Execution as a Decision-making Process, https://www.henricodolfing.com/2018/10/strategy-execution-as-decision-making.htmlOctober 21, 2018
12. https://www.goodreads.com/quotes/1007201
13. Admin, Grievance Management, simplinotes.com,

Grievance Management, 1 March, 2019
14. Aniruddha S.; Grievance Management: Introduction, forms, procedure and management; economicdiscussion.net
15. https://www.brainyquote.com/quotes/jack_lew_442942
16. Akhilesh Ganti, https://www.investopedia.com/terms/b/budget.asp, 18 March, 2021
17. Jason Fernando,https://www.investopedia.com/terms/a/accounting.asp, 18 Feb., 2021.
18. economictimes.indiatimes.com/definition/audit
19. https://www.investindia.gov.in/taxation
20. https:/cleartax.in/s/income-tax-raid, Income Tax Raid, Search and Seizure–What, When, How, 4 Jan., 2021
21. A. Bhardawaj: What is Marketing Management; A Bhardawaj; economicdiscussion.netsuccess.com
22. https://www.unleashedsoftware.com/blog/purchase-management-matter,What is purchase management: what it is and why does it matter? 2 Sep., 2019
23. What is contract management; National Contracts Management Association; ncmahq.org
24. https://investedwallet.com/top-finance-quotes/
25. managementstudyguide.com/financial management
26. https://www.azquotes.com/author/7900-John_F_Kennedy/tag/water
27. Hemant Singh: jagranjosh.com/general knowledge: Water Management: Meaning, Statistics and Solutions, 7 Sep., 2019
28. https://www.azquotes.com/quotes/topics/solid-waste.html
29. Dr, SureshHaware: *In Service of Sai*, Prabhat Prakashan New Delhi, Feb. 2021
30. https://in.pinterest.com/pin/30328997465190054/
31. James Sinopoli: sciencedirect.com; Electric power management systems; *in: Smart Building systems for Architects, Owners and Builders*, 2015

32. David Stephen, *in: Independent Generation of Electrical Power*, 1994
33. sumologic.com/glossary/infrastructure-management; Sumo Logic
34. https://www.practicealchemy.com/blog/50-inspirational-quotes-for-lawyers
35. bluescreen.pt; Blue Screen IT solutions; *Legal Management System: Smarter Legal Tech Solution*
36. https://www.goodreads.com/author/quotes/4627172.Sachin_Tendulkar
37. 'What is technology management?', *Journal of Technology Management*, vol. 2, no. 1, publisher: Emerald Group Publishing Limited; 2007, emerald.com; Emerald Group Publishing Limited
38. https://pt.slideshare.net/geovrakas/10-inspirational-quotes-for-successful-procurement-and-contract-management-by-george-vrakas
39. https://www.brainyquote.com/authors/a-p-j-abdul-kalam-quotes
40. https://www.quotemaster.org/end+world+hunger
41. https://www.goodreads.com/author/quotes/4627172.Sachin_Tendulkar
42. iNurture.co.in, *Accommodation management–An Important Role in Hospitality Business*
43. https://www.scoonews.com/news/10-inspiring-educational-quotes-by-mahatma-gandhi-10305
44. https://www.saramarberry.com/10-more-inspirational-quotes-for-healthcare-design/
45. https://gearnixe.com/blood-donation-quotes-images/
46. https://www.trvst.world/foa/waste-recycling/waste-quotes/
47. https://www.helpscout.com/customer-service-quotes/inspirational/
48. https://www.southernliving.com/culture/unity-quotes
49. https://www.brainyquote.com/quotes/lao_tzu_137141

□

Appendix-1

Glimpse of
The Shri Saibaba Sansthan Trust (Shirdi) Act 2004

GOVERNMENT OF MAHARASHTRA LAW AND JUDICIARY DEPARTMENT
MAHARASHTRA ACT No. XIV OF 2004
THE SHREE SAI BABA SANSTHAN TRUST (SHIRDI) ACT, 2004
(As modified upto the 22nd April, 2013)

Here are some of the provisions of the above said Act. For details, you may obtain the full Act from the government website.

Contents of the Act Book

9. Disqualification for memberhisp.
10. Power to appoint new member.
11. Meeting of Committee and rules of procedure.
12. Act of Committee not invalid by reason of vacancy or defect.
13. Executive Officer and other officers of Committee.
14. Powers and duties of officers of Committee.
15. Terms and conditions of service of Executive Officer and other officers and employees.
16. Allocation of employees of public trust to Sansthan Trust.
17. Duties and powers of Committee.
18. Advisory Council.
19. *Bhakta Mandal.*
20. Trust Fund.
21. Utilization of Trust Fund.
22. Management Fund and its utilisation.
23. Suits and other proceedings by or against Trust or Committee.
24. Continuance of legal proceedings by or against erstwhile public trust and construction of references to that Trust.
25. Rules.
26. Power of state government to give directions, call for report, documents, etc.
27. Inspection by government.
28. Power of state government to call for record, etc.
29. Annual Report of Committee.
30. Power of state government to suspend or rescind any resolution or order, etc., of Committee in certain cases.
31. Members of Committee and officers and employees of Trust to be public servants.
32. Protection of action taken in good faith.
33. Act to override other laws, etc.
34. Dissolution and supersession of Committee.
35. Removal of difficulties.

Provisions Regarding the Appointment of Trustees

(*2*) The state government shall, by notification in the *Official Gazette,* appoint, a chairman, vice chairman and not more than 1[fifteen] other members to constitute the Committee as envisaged under sub-section (*1*):

Provided that, out of the total number of members not less than one member shall be a woman and one member shall be from the socially and economically weaker sections.

[Provided further that, out of the total number of members, not less than eight members including the vice chairman, shall be persons having educational background with professional or specialised knowledge, qualifications and practical experience in one or more of the fields, such as law, Business Management, Public Administration, Engineering, Architecture, Public Health, Medicine or Rural Development.]

(*3*) The president of the Shirdi *Nagar Panchayat* shall be the *ex-officio* member of the Committee.

(*4*) Subject to the other provisions of this Act, the Committee shall be a body corporate by the name aforesaid, having perpetual succession and a common seal with power to acquire, hold and dispose of property, both movable and immovable, and to contract and shall by the said name sue and be sued.

Honorarium, etc.

6. (*1*) These shall be paid from the Management Fund to each member such honorarium, fees and allowances as the chairman, vice chairman or as the case may be, member of the Committee, as may be determined by the state government, from time to time.

Disqualification of Member

(*3*) If a member without obtaining leave from the Committee, remains absent for the three consecutive meetings of the Committee, he shall cease to be a member thereof, from the time the third meeting is duly terminated.

Meeting of Committee and Rules of Procedure

11. (*1*) For the transaction of its business, the Committee shall meet at such intervals as it may determine, from time to time, so however, that not more than thirty days shall elapse between the two meetings.

(*2*) The quorum for the meeting of the Committee shall be 1[eight].

(*3*) Every meeting of the Committee shall be presided over by the chairman and in his absence by the vice chairman and in their absence, by a member elected for the purpose by the members present.

(*4*) All questions arising at the meeting of the Committee shall be determined by the majority of the votes of the members present. In the case of equality of votes, the chairman or the person presiding, as the case may be, shall have a right to exercise a casting vote.

(*5*) The Executive Officer appointed under section 13 shall be the secretary of the Committee and shall be responsible for the maintenance of the minutes of the proceedings of every meeting duly countersigned by the chairman or any other member presiding at the meeting.

The Act has to be obeyed in letter and spirit. The Act prevails over any circulars, if there is a conflict, even if it is issued after the Act is published.

□

Appendix-2

Purchase Procedure

Maharashtra government has approved the purchase procedure for all the government offices, corporations, government departments vide a Government Regulation GR dated 30th October, 2015 (latest) and is applicable for the purchase by Shri Sai Baba Sansthan Trust, Shirdi. Every temple will follow its own procedure but such procedure has to be in place for the purpose of transparency. Salient features of this procedure are given here in brief. For details one can obtain the full document from the website of the government of Maharashtra.

Objective

The purpose of this regulation is to present the least expensive process for the purchase of goods. It is also aimed to have a common, transparent, systematic and efficient procedure for the purchase by all the government departments.

Scope

It is limited to the purchase of goods and not applicable for the services or establishments. It is also not applicable to the purchases by the Directorate of Information and Technology Department.

Principles of Purchase

It is expected that the money vested with the government by the public and taxpayers should be judiciously spent and the public at large shall be assured that the money is being spent for achieving the intended objectives to benefit the needy ones. The following principles shall be on the top of the thought while making a purchase.

1. Optimum or ideal value for money
2. Honesty and transparency
3. Sufficient competition
4. Long-term benefits
5. Sustainable purchase policy and
6. Ways to arrest corrupt practices

Applying these principles the purchaser should ensure that there is no wastage of purchased goods. There is a review process to overlook upon the purchase made by various departments of the government.

It is necessary to purchase ISI standard quality products. It should be ensured from the Bureau of Indian Standards (BIS) that the particular product is certified by the institution. Also the reasonableness of the price shall be established. Taxes and fees shall be properly calculated and paid to the concerned departments. Encouragement shall be given to the startup businesses.

Types of Purchase

The concerned officer shall assess the need and decide the type of purchase procedure to be followed from among the following ones. Based on the urgency and the value of the purchase, the type is normally decided by the purchase officer. Each type of purchase procedure has its advantages and disadvantages. Also there are limitations and permissions to be obtained in some cases. Details will be available in the above said GR.

1. Open competitive tender
2. On the spot purchase

3. Purchase based on standard item rate card
4. Limited tender purchase
5. Purchase from the suppliers on panel
6. Singular source purchase
7. Swiss challenge procedure
8. Purchase by expression of interest

It is mandatory that any item costing above Rs. 3 lakhs shall be purchased through the process of e-tendering. There is also a procedure defined for the purchase of goods during emergency situations.

Tendering

For the goods costing above Rs. 3 lakhs e-tendering has been made mandatory. It has to be done using the e-portal of the government of Maharashtra. Sometimes two envelope systems are also followed for the purchase of goods. Tender notice shall be issued in the newspaper and also published on the e-portal. Sai Sansthan, in addition, publishes all its purchase notices on the website of Sansthan. There is a guideline regarding publication of the tender notice. Depending upon the value of the tender and the type of goods the notice can be issued either in local newspapers or district newspapers or state-level or national-level newspapers. Cost of the tender document and the earnest money deposit to be taken from the tenderer is also specified. The tender notice shall give the commencement date of the sale of tender document, closing date, pre-bid meeting if any, tender opening date, earnest money deposit and its process etc. The tenders are required to be opened in the presence of all the vendors. The lowest quote has to be selected for offering the purchase order. He is called L-1. If he is not willing to supply the goods then the offer goes to L-2 and so on. If you do not get at least three offers then the item has to be re-tendered. In this case even if you get two valid offers you can choose the supplier and place the purchase order upon him. If you do not get two valid offers then the item has to be again re-tendered for the third time. Here even if you get one valid offer the supplier can be selected.

Purchase Order

On selection of the supplier, the purchase order shall be placed upon him. It is a legal document and should be properly prepared in consultation with the legal department. Payment conditions is an important clause of the purchase order. This is the clause through which you can regulate the purchase.

Acceptance of Goods

Immediately upon receipt of the goods the same shall be inspected as per the acceptance criteria. The shortfalls shall be communicated to the supplier and if he is willing to fulfil/rectify the same then the goods shall be accepted after fulfilling the conditions of the supply.

Blacklisting

There is a procedure given for blacklisting of the suppliers who have failed to comply with the purchase order or failed in supplying the quality goods.

Grievance Cell

It is suggested to have a grievance cell to listen to the vendors or public and resolve the same as soon as possible.

Thus the purchase procedure published by the government of Maharashtra is the guideline for the Sai Sansthan for its purchases. It has to be followed meticulously. In my opinion the guideline is very good and it is advisable that even the sufficiently grown up private companies can follow such a procedure and get benefitted out of it.

□

Appendix-3

Contracts Procedure

Similar to the purchase procedure there is a procedure laid down by the government of Maharashtra for getting the works done through the process of contracts. *Government Regulation* published by the Public Works Department of the government of Maharashtra on 27th September, 2018 is the latest one followed at Sai Sansthan, Shirdi. Following are the brief provisions of the contracts and for details the full document can be obtained from the website of the government of Maharashtra:

Contracts are normally given for the construction works which are taking relatively longer time durations. It could be the making/repairs of roads, buildings, sheds, etc. The government of Maharashtra has issued the guidelines for execution of such works, based on the long experience of the Public Works Department.

e-Tender Notice

For the works costing more than Rs. 3 lakhs, the works shall be awarded through the process of e-tendering and the one whose quotation is lowest shall be awarded the contract. For the works costing less than Rs. 3 lakhs, the tender notice shall be published on the notice-board of Sansthan for eight days and if there is no response, the same shall be published again for next three days. Other works shall be executed through the tender notice published in the newspapers as per the following guidelines:

1.	Rs. 3 to 500 lakhs	1 district level Marathi and 2 state level newspapers
2.	Rs. 5 to 25 cr	1 district level Marathi and 2 state level and 2 national papers
3.	Above Rs. 25 cr	2 district level 5 state level and 4 national level newspapers
4.	Rs. 100 cr	4 district level 6 state level and 4 national level newspapers

Notice Period

Minimum period of notice shall be as follows:

1.	3 to 50 lakhs	15 days for 1st time, 10 days 2nd time and 7 days 3rd time
2.	5 to 25 cr	25 days for 1st time, 15 days 2nd time and 10 days 3rd time
3.	25 to 100 cr	25 days for 1st time, 25 days 2nd time and 15 days 3rd time
4.	Above 100 cr	45 days for 1st time, 30 days 2nd time and 15 days 3rd time

The days above said are inclusive of the holidays.

E-tender Categories

There is a prescription for various types of tendering systems depending upon the cost of the works and there are also the level of authorities who will approve the tenders. There are details regarding pre bid meetings to be organised for works costing more than Rs. 1.5 crores and corrections if required to be incorporated in the tender document along with earnest money deposit, security deposit, registration of contractors, cost escalation clause, etc.

Opening e-tender

There are detailed instructions regarding opening of the e-tender, the activities to be completed before opening the tender, things to be done while opening the tender, e.g. attendance of the bidders, etc. If two envelope system is followed, then after opening the first envelope containing the technical bid, the eligibility of the bidders shall be communicated to all the bidders with the reasons and the same shall be published on the website of the government of Maharashtra and Sansthan. If there are any objections of the bidders who are not eligible and they want to complain, then the same shall be properly redressed, published on the web and then only the second envelope containing the commercial bid shall be opened in presence of the eligible bidders.

Acceptance of Offer

L-1 offer shall be accepted. If he is not ready, then L-2 should be accepted and so on. There are conditions prescribed if the offer is more than the estimated cost by 10 per cent and above or if the offer is less than the estimated cost by 15 per cent and above. Additional performance security deposit, validity period of the acceptance of tender, refund of EMD of the bidders other than L-1 and L-2 etc. get involved.

There are two types of tenders, viz. Item rate tender and fixed-cost tender. The taxes shall be properly paid during the execution of the works. In my opinion it is preferred to follow the process of fixed cost tender rather than the item rate tender as it has the provision to escalate the total cost of the work which could be misused for misappropriation.

The work order for the contract is a legal document and therefore it should be properly prepared in consultation with the legal department. Since it is a long-term contract the clauses like arbitration, delay penalty, incentive if completing the work early shall be properly drafted. There could be a clause stating that the CEO of Sansthan shall be the sole arbitrator and his decision shall be binding on the contractors. Though this does not prohibit him from approaching the courts but serves the purpose in most of the cases because not everyone will go to the court.

I think the provisions are sufficiently elaborated and good enough to execute the job in the intended manner.

□□□